SIGNS OF

WARNING

SIGNS OF

HOPE

SEVEN COMING CRISES THAT WILL CHANGE YOUR LIFE

SIGNS OF
WARNING
SIGNS OF
HOPE

SEVEN COMING CRISES THAT WILL CHANGE YOUR LIFE

J. KERBY ANDERSON

MOODY PRESS
CHICAGO

© 1994 by
J. KERBY ANDERSON

All Scripture quotations, unless indicated, are taken from the *New American Standard Bible*, © 1960, 1962, 1963, 1968, 1971, 1972, 1973, 1975, 1977 by The Lockman Foundation. Used by permission.

ISBN: 0-8024-7835-2

1 3 5 7 9 10 8 6 4 2

Printed in the United States of America

CONTENTS

ACKNOWLEDGMENTS

Writing a book can be a long, tedious, often frustrating process. Some have compared it to pregnancy and birth. If so, this was one of the longer, more difficult book pregnancies on record.

Five earlier books did not prepare me for the experience of writing this one. A project begun in 1989 and finally put into print in 1994 was obviously a tedious and sometimes discouraging process—full of many dead ends. And in the midst of the tedium were as many twists and turns as a roller coaster. Somehow, someway, the ride is now coming to an end. I have simultaneous feelings of relief and accomplishment.

This book originally began with a co-author. I thank Rob McEnany for his early involvement in this project. I would never have considered making the long trek through demographic data without a trusted guide who travels those familiar paths every day as an advertising executive. Although it ended up being a solitary path, I appreciate him helping me become a pioneer in a whole new academic area.

I also want to thank the editors at Moody Press for their willingness to rescue a manuscript that I concluded would probably never get published. Their desire to publish a revised, reworked, rewritten manuscript kept me going and allowed me to finally finish this book. And their willingness to navigate the legal thicket of contracts and competing claims made this book possible.

Finally, I would like to thank my family, friends, and colleagues who periodically asked about the book and kept encouraging me even when there was no encouraging news to report. Thank you for believing in me and this project.

INTRODUCTION

T he baby boom generation is on a collision course with the twenty-first century. Yet the members of this vast cohort are only beginning to recognize the early signs of this impending confrontation with reality and seem ill-prepared to cope when it does occur.

The stage is set for a series of impending crises. The seventy-six million boomers, born between the years of 1946 and 1964, are approaching midlife and are certain to experience some in-flight turbulence before the 1990s have run their course. Changing social and economic conditions are also affecting them as well as the generations preceding and following them. Whether you were born within the baby boom or not, these coming crises are certain to change your life.

Before we continue, allow me to clarify a key point. I do not use the word *crisis* solely in the negative sense. Although there are various dictionary definitions for crisis (both positive and negative), we tend to view the English word only in a negative context. Compare our colloquial definition to the Chinese word for crisis, which is composed of two picture-characters—one means "danger" whereas the other means "opportunity." I believe that the coming changes present a crisis in both senses of the word.

For most of us, facing a crisis means trouble or failure. It is a testimony of our inability to cope or mount a challenge. Certainly that is one definition of crisis. But throughout this book, I hope you will remind yourself of the other legitimate definition of the word. A crisis can be a turning point, a point of transition, or an adjustment to changing social and cultural circumstances.

Aware of our society's negative reaction to the word *crisis,* Gail Sheehy substituted a more ambiguous and inert term—*passages*—in her best-selling book. The term was appropriate for a book dealing solely with psychological passages. This book, however, is broader in scope and considers sociological, economic, and spiritual issues as well as psychological ones. Thus, *crisis* is the term I use to describe the momentous changes taking place in the 1990s and into the twenty-first century.

Social commentators writing about the crises facing us in the next few decades have often used an illustration or metaphor from meteorology. They talk of "weathering a storm" or facing a hurricane. But I would suggest that a more apt analogy can be found in geology (or more precisely, seismology).

Geologists tell us that the continents of the world ride upon massive tectonic plates that move imperceptibly year after year. These subtle movements build up enormous pressures along fault lines, eventually leading to devastating earthquakes within those fault zones.

Predicting an earthquake is much more difficult than predicting a hurricane. Our abilities to do so are (pardon the pun) faulty at best. Seismologists can measure the movement of these plates, and they can tell us that an earthquake will come eventually, but they cannot, with any precision, tell us when or where an earthquake will hit.

That is an apt metaphor for the crises surrounding the baby boom generation. It has been part of one of the largest generations in history and has made an impact on the rest of society. Whereas some of the changes have been sudden, most have been gradual and imperceptible. Like tectonic plates beneath the culture, the subtle changes are building up pressures along the fault lines of society.

The analogy breaks down, however, on one key point. We are unable to alter the size, location, and timing of an earthquake.

Seismologists can measure the movement of tectonic plates, but they can do nothing to halt their inexorable progress toward destruction. They can tell us that an earthquake is coming but must wait helplessly for "the big one" to hit.

By contrast, I believe that we can alter the direction and force of many of these coming crises. Most social changes, like tectonic plates, are difficult to perceive. We need help in recognizing the changes and crises that are subtly changing our lives. Unlike tectonic plates, the impact of such changes can be altered. Advance warning can help us build stronger foundations to ride out the tremors and shocks that will accompany their collision with our lives.

Indeed, one of the themes of this book is reminiscent of the TV commercial for auto repairs: "pay me now or pay me later." Deal with the crises now, or experience a devastating earthquake later. Pay attention to the social, psychological, economic, and spiritual tremors now or face a crisis of seismic proportions later.

The baby boom generation, in particular, appears to be the brunt of a perverse "good news/bad news" joke. The very factors that defined and distinguished it in its early years may be the instruments of its undoing. Its enormous size, its different values, and its cultural clout changed the world. Now its members and the whole of society are finding it difficult to cope with that changing world.

This book is born of the conviction that this generation has within it the intellectual, emotional, and spiritual resources necessary to face the coming crises. We begin with a backward look to explore and understand the cultural context, economic circumstances, and decisive events that have affected this generation. Subsequent chapters define and describe the future crises likely to influence us both individually and collectively.

Although these chapters provide some solutions and recommended reading, let me hasten to add that the number of solutions are few. The reason is twofold. First, the baby boom generation does not allow for a "one size fits all" kind of answer. The advice someone would give to a forty-five-year-old married man would be different from what someone would give a thirty-year-old single woman. One is dealing with an empty nest and may find himself in the midst of the "sandwich generation." The other is struggling with loneliness or disillusionment. Differences in age, gender, marital status, family situation, and so on preclude a simple answer that would cover the diversity within the baby boom generation.

Second, solutions can only come once one clearly understands the problem. Over the last few years I have developed a
list of sayings known to my radio listeners as "Anderson's Axi-
oms." One of the most common is: Beware of the person who
readily prescribes solutions before he truly understands the problem. The rash of self-help books on the market today testifies to
the shallow thinking and analysis of the writers. This book is
long on diagnosis and short on prescription. I believe that once
you understand the problem, you can begin to devise your own
individual solution to the crises that will inevitably affect your
life.

This book does attempt to provide information and insight
that will enable you to discover why you have arrived at a particular circumstance. You should have hope because knowing a
transition is coming will help you anticipate the changes and react accordingly. Moreover, knowing that you are not alone in experiencing these transitions will give you a sense of comfort and
opportunity to find support.

The message of *Signs of Warning, Signs of Hope* is straightfor-
ward: You can confront and alter the impact of the coming crises
on your life. You are not impotent to affect the subterranean tectonic trends in our culture. You can make a difference if you are
forearmed and forewarned about the coming changes that will
affect your life.

SECTION ONE

THE BABY BOOM GENERATION

CHAPTER ONE
THE BABY BOOM GENERATION

T hough it began with a bang, most people thought it would end with a whimper. A record number of births were recorded nine months after V-J Day and every month thereafter. By the end of the year, an all-time U.S. record had been set with 3.4 million births.

But that was just the beginning. Demographers expected the boom in babies to taper off quickly as merely a post-war phenomenon. But it did not end as it did in Europe. Instead, a bumper crop of more than three million babies was born the next year and the following year. The number increased to four million births in 1954 and continued for eleven straight years through 1964. By the time the tidal wave of births had washed over the landscape, a total of seventy-six million children had been added to the American population.

The unprecedented number of births caught both experts and laypeople by surprise. Demographers had predicted a decline in the U.S. birthrate following World War II and even stuck to their predictions during the early years of the baby boom. Finally, though, the evidence was clear: the American decline in fertility had been thrown into reverse, at least temporarily.

America's population explosion during those nineteen years was not due to decreased mortality as was the case with many less developed countries. It was the by-product of increased fertility. The generation preceding the baby boom generation was smaller and part of a long-term decline in fertility rates. The fertility rate in the 1930s averaged roughly 2.1 births per woman. By contrast, the fertility rate during the height of the baby boom (late 1950s) reached 3.7 births per woman.[1]

When the baby boom ended, the decline in fertility resumed. The generation following the baby boom has, since the mid-1970s, had a fertility rate of 1.8 births per woman. In essence, the baby boom was a time of exceptional and unprecedented reproduction in the midst of reproductive decline. The Population Reference Bureau in Washington, D.C., explained the birth phenomenon this way: "Simply put, the baby boom was a 'disturbance' which emanated from a decade-and-a-half fertility splurge on the part of American couples. This post–World War II phenomenon upset what had been a century-long decline in the U.S. fertility rate."[2]

The baby boom became a generational sandwich not unlike those made by the comic strip character Dagwood. The boomers were the bulging middle between two thin slices of generations that preceded and followed them: the baby bust of their parents in the 1930s and the baby bust of their children in the 1980s and 1990s.

Surrounded as they were by smaller generations on both sides, the baby boom stood out in both numbers and influence. Sociologists frequently use the metaphor of a "pig in a python" to describe the expansion and contraction of its influence as this generation moves through its various life stages. As the pig has traveled through the python, it has had a considerable influence on both pig and python.

EARLY IMPACT

The relentless arrival of millions of babies into the world each year created an instant demand for baby products.[3] Diaper industry revenues nearly doubled, from $32 million in 1947 to $50 million by 1957. Diaper services also prospered, as did sales of bassinets, playpens, and high chairs. By 1953, more than 1.5 billion cans of baby food were being consumed each year.

The Baby Boom

Millions of Births

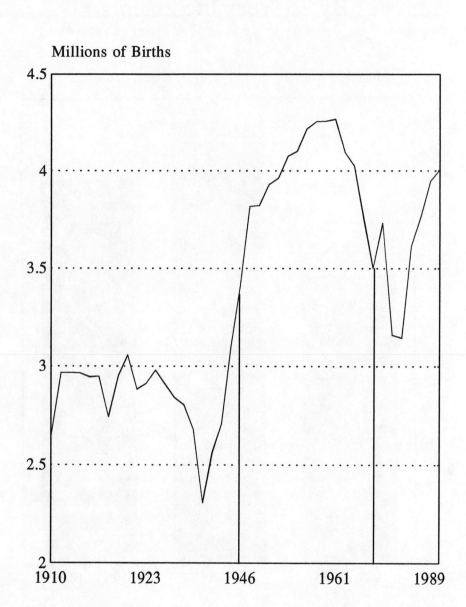

Source: U.S. Census Bureau.

Number of Births
By 19-Year Increments

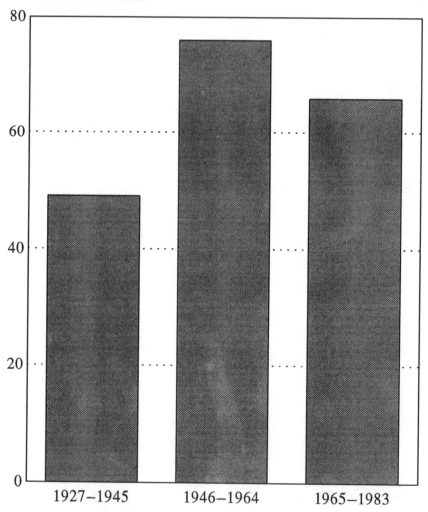

Millions of births

Source: U.S. Center for Health Statistics.

Parents looking for advice turned a relatively obscure paper-back by Dr. Benjamin Spock into an international best-seller. Dr. Spock had the good fortune of publishing *The Common Sense Book of Baby and Child Care* a month after the baby boom began, in 1946. The thirty-five-cent Pocket Books edition sold four million copies by 1952 and at least one million a year for eighteen years after that.[4] Dr. Spock's book launched the baby boom generation, at least psychologically. Parents reared on the adage "children should be seen but not heard" were reassured by Dr. Spock that they should follow their instincts and provide love, care, and comfort for their babies. He came out for demand feeding and encouraged parents to strive to meet the needs of their children.

Although his only "fault" may have been that he dispensed helpful advice in a sympathetic manner, Dr. Spock became associated with "permissiveness." When he revised his book in 1957, he adopted a stricter philosophy, but it was too late.[5] The public perception of Dr. Spock and his progeny was fixed. The baby boom generation came to be known as "Spock babies." When Dr. Spock joined the antiwar movement in the 1960s, the label became an epithet used to describe the early years of a generation.

In reality, the Spock connection has been exaggerated. The mind-set of the boom generation during its formative years was much more focused on the unique situation in which boomers found themselves than on Dr. Spock. As we will elaborate in the next chapter, this generation grew up in a time of affluence, optimism, and opportunity. Medical advances and economic expansion, coupled with parental desires to rear a generation of healthy and wealthy children, gave this generation a feeling that it was special and destined for greatness.

> The message was not lost on the baby boomers. They, too, knew that they were special. Their parents had endlessly told them how fortunate they were. Their experience provided ample proof of their specialness: they'd had new schools, crisp new schoolbooks every year, homes so new that the putty was barely dry, toys of gleaming plastic. Their whole world was fraught with the promise and fresh smell of a new car. They were at home in the culture of the new.[6]

This was hardly the first generation to believe such a claim. But no other generation has believed it with greater confidence and

The Number of Baby Boomers

How many boomers are there? Well, there were 75,873,000
live births between 1946 and 1964 in the U.S. But there are
now estimated to be 77,268,000 boomers. The increase is due
to immigration.

Source: *The Boomer Report*, April 1989, 8.

conviction. Boomers were special and ready to make an impact
on society.

Their impact on the consumer market was demonstrated
throughout the 1950s. It started with baby products and soon
was felt in other areas of the economy.

When Fess Parker donned a Davy Crockett coonskin cap in
1955, young boomers first demonstrated the economic clout of
their generation. "The Ballad of Davy Crockett," by Bill Hayes,
moved to the top of the charts and was translated into sixteen
languages. More than three thousand Davy Crockett items, including lunch pails, toothbrushes, and sweatshirts, accounted for
more than $100 million in sales. And the wholesale price of rac-
coon skins jumped from twenty-six cents a pound to eight dollars
a pound.[7]

In 1958, two enterprising entrepreneurs imported an idea
from Australia. Their Wham-O Corporation began to manufac-
ture simple plastic hoops they called Hula-Hoops. Boomers went
berserk. By year's end, as many as twenty thousand hoops were
being produced each day in order to keep up with the demand.[8]
But in 1959 the market collapsed when baby boomers suddenly
declared Hula-Hoops passé.

That wasn't the last time boomers defined a fad or trend and
then turned their back on it. Marketers have come to appreciate
the fickle nature of this generation's tastes and appetites. When
the editors of *Time* decided to wish the first baby boomers a happy fortieth birthday, they described this generation's penchant
for change.

Hopping from one instant fad to another—from Davy Crockett
coonskin caps to Hula-Hoops—they moved as a single mass,
conditioned to think alike and do alike. Trendiness became a

generation hallmark: from pot to yoga to jogging, they embraced the In thing of the moment and then quickly chucked it for another.[9]

Whether as babies, toddlers, youth, or adults, the baby boom generation has profoundly changed the life stage it entered and forced society to take notice of it. When boomers buy alike, they change the consumer market. And when they think alike, they change the popular culture.

THE YOUTH CULTURE

The arrival of the oldest baby boomers on the doorstep of the public school system was the first evidence of the generation's "pig in the python" effect on society. Their appearance put the first of what would be many public institutions on overload. Between 1950 and 1970, elementary school enrollment rose by two-thirds. The tidal wave of births just a few years earlier was now washing onto the public school system with overwhelming force.

To make matters worse, that wave hit, almost unexpectedly, in the early 1950s with a force of a tsunami. The class of students born in 1946 and 1947 was more than one-third larger than the preceding class. For the next twelve years, each graduating senior class was replaced by an ensuing wave of kindergartners that outnumbered it by an average of 1.5 million students.[10]

That sudden arrival of students affected both pig and python. The public education system immediately hit overload. School districts scrambled to build more schools and hire more teachers. But each year brought an additional increase in students, so the public school system could not catch up until the last baby boomers were finishing school. Then there was a surplus of schools and teachers.

But the greatest effect may have been on members of the baby boom generation themselves. They turned out to be the best educated generation in history. Yet that statistic relates only to quantity, not quality. Although the average baby boomer has spent more years in school than any generation preceding it or following it, many wonder about the quality of that education. A generation filled with optimism, idealism, and great promise probably didn't get the education it deserved, because there were simply too many children to educate in too little time.

Differences Between Generations

	PARENTS	BOOMERS
Shaping events	Great Depression World War II	Vietnam Watergate
View of government	Solves problems	Causes problems
Social view	Conservative, status quo	Tolerant of change, more liberal
Issues	Economy, war and peace	Economy, environment, family
Singer	Frank Sinatra	Bruce Springsteen
Television show	"Father Knows Best"	"thirtysomething"
Car	Chevrolet, Ford	BMW, Honda, Toyota
Dread disease	Polio	AIDS
View of Soviets	Cold War	Glasnost
Admired foreign leader	Winston Churchill	Mikhail Gorbachev

Adapted from a chart that appeared in the *Dallas Morning News*.

Moreover, the bumper crop of children making their way through an educational system running on overload created what we call today "the youth culture." Certainly one of the legacies of the baby boom generation is the way it changed the socialization process not only in America but throughout most of the Western world.

The goal of society in general, and of education in particular, is to pass its culture on from the older generation to the younger.

But the boom in birth dramatically changed the ratio between children and parents as well as between students and teachers. That disparity made it virtually impossible to communicate the core values, the ancient verities of past generations, successfully.

The passage from child to adult was being delayed into a time of extended adolescence—a previously unrecognized stage of life that psychologist Kenneth Keniston simply called "youth." The boom generation found itself in a world of its own. In grade school, boomers' overworked and overwhelmed teachers were frequently just trying to cope with the task of educating so many. By junior high school and high school, students no longer had the continuity of one teacher for every class. So they began to look to each other for direction and support. Instead of looking to adults for guidance, they created their own world. They had their own music, their own fashions, their own language, and their own rules. The social threads that bind different generations together were beginning to unravel. Soon adults and children alike were talking about a generation gap.

That gap widened due to both demographics and psychographics. The demographic difference for a generation gap was fairly obvious: baby boomers outnumbered their parents. Each generation faces the task of transmitting the culture to the next generation, which arrives on the scene like a horde of barbarians. The task of the older generation is to control the "invasion of barbarians" and focus their zeal and energy toward becoming contributors to society.[11]

By the time the boom of births had ended in the mid-1960s, the barbarians of the boom outnumbered their cultural mentors and quickly overwhelmed those guarding society's gate. Instead of society's placing its stamp on them, they began to place their stamp on society.

The psychographic reason for a generation gap was twofold: education and media. Part of the generation gap was an education gap. Eighty-five percent of leading-edge baby boomers (those born from 1947 to 1951) completed high school, whereas only 38 percent of their parents did.[12] And whereas a majority of boomers went on to college, only a small minority of their parents had done so. The gap widened as the two generations began to think differently.

Second, because of the difference in media exposure, boomers and their parents perceived the world differently. Baby boomers were the first TV generation. They grew up in a global

Differences Within
the Baby Boom Generation

	BORN AROUND 1946	BORN AROUND 1958
TV series	"Father Knows Best"	"The Partridge Family"
Kiddie show	"Howdy Doody"	"Romper Room"
Toy	Mr. Potato Head (with a real potato)	Mr. Potato Head (all plastic version)
Runner-up toy	The Hula-Hoop	G. I. Joe
Goopy stuff	Garden variety mud	Play-Doh
Singing family	The Everly Brothers	The Jackson 5
Transportation	Scooters	Skateboards
Monsters	Godzilla, King Kong	"The Munsters"
Cartoon	"Mighty Mouse"	"The Flintstones"
Comic book heroes	Superman	Batman
Sports heroes	Jackie Robinson	Hank Aaron
Female role model	Annette Funicello of "The Mouseketeers"	Stephanie Powers in "The Girl from U.N.C.L.E."

Adapted from chart in *USA Weekend*, August 19–21, 1988.

village.[13] Their horizons and perspectives were broadened as they were exposed to different cultures, traditions, ideas, and values —all through the new entertainment-information medium in their living rooms.

For most boomers, television was "the first curriculum." When it wasn't teaching them facts, it was conveying values by opening up new vistas for exploration. It became a primary vehicle for transmitting culture, usurping the role parents and teachers had played in previous generations.

The sheer numbers of the boom generation not only created a generation gap; they also reversed the flow of cultural influence. In previous generations, fads and fashions were like raindrops washing down from older age groups to younger. But as the boom generation began to dominate the youth culture, trends and fashions began to bubble up like springs and frequently erupted like geysers. Children of the boom were the trendsetters. They rejected the roles, values, lifestyles, and institutions of the previous generation and imposed their language (buzzwords and slogans), fashions (hair, clothes), and lifestyle on the culture. They defined what was in vogue and what was out.

Not only did parents begin to take their cues from the boom generation, but so did later generations of young people. The boom generation became the dominant youth culture when it was young, as well as when it became older. As a result, one of the boom industries in the 1970s and 1980s was nostalgia. Even children who were not alive during the 1950s eagerly sang Beach Boys songs and watched "Happy Days" and "Laverne and Shirley." Likewise, children born after the 1960s still reveled in Beatles songs and rarely missed the latest episode of "The Wonder Years."

CHILDREN OF THE SIXTIES

It is hardly an exaggeration to say that the baby boom generation was profoundly affected by the events of the 1960s. Nowhere is that better illustrated than in a poll published in *Rolling Stone* magazine. Anticipating a watershed election in 1988, the editors of the magazine commissioned Peter D. Hart Research Associates to conduct an extensive survey of Americans aged eighteen to forty-four. Their results provided a "portrait of a generation" (somewhat larger than the baby boom generation) that covered various "aspects of their lives, from political preferences to private morality, from economic anxieties to social ideals."[14]

The survey proved what many social commentators had been saying for a long time. The generation is not easily labeled, and it is dramatically diverse. Whereas 18 percent of those surveyed said they pursued a counterculture lifestyle in the 1960s, 30 percent said they opposed the rebels of their own generation.

Yet in the midst of that diversity there were experiences and attitudes that bound this generation together and set it apart from generations that preceded it. Unlike previous generations, baby boomers do not have one formative experience (such as the Great Depression or World War II) that defines them. Instead, the boom generation is defined by a set of experiences.

According to the poll, the "turbulence of the sixties was the formative experience" for this generation.[15] In particular, two events stand out: the civil rights movement and the Vietnam War. In fact, those events were influential even for those boomers too young to have participated in marches or protests or to have served in combat. Those two pivotal events gave this generation its idealism and its cynicism. The civil rights movement was the source of its idealism and forged the ideals of tolerance and equality evident to this day. It was a cause worth joining, and it energized youthful imagination if not action. On the other hand, the Vietnam War provided this generation with its cynicism. Nearly half of baby boomers knew someone who was wounded or killed in Vietnam. But unlike their parents who took strength and renewed resolve from World War II casualties, baby boomers were disillusioned by the Vietnam War. Consequently, they have led a movement toward an isolationist view of foreign policy.

Even more important than their experiences are their heroes. Although their heroes are dead, their memories live on in the minds of the baby boom generation as motivating ideals. When asked by the poll to name two people they most admired, they did not select a president, a captain of industry, or even a contemporary figure. Their first choice was a black Baptist preacher murdered twenty years earlier: Martin Luther King, Jr. Their second choice was a young senator also assassinated in 1968: Robert F. Kennedy.[16] Those two men stood for the values most revered by this generation, and they have been venerated by their martyrdom. The King and Kennedy connection links this generation to the bipolar nature of its experiences. Its heroes stood for the ideals of love, peace, justice, and tolerance. Yet both were killed before their dreams could be realized.

As we will discuss, one recurring theme for baby boomers is their striving for ideals with heightened expectations and their falling into disillusionment when those goals prove illusory. This generation that grew up expecting too much has had to face disappointment.

Woodstock, Watergate, the Vietnam War, and the assassinations of John Kennedy, Martin Luther King, Jr., Robert Kennedy, and John Lennon have all had their impact on baby boomers. But even more important than the events themselves is the medium that influenced them. Because baby boomers were the first television generation, no other generation experienced such pivotal events in such an immediate and collective way. Through television, baby boomers witnessed the landing of the Beatles on American soil and the landing of Americans on lunar soil; the fall of soldiers in Vietnam and the fall of politicians in Watergate.

In fact, television was more than just the source of vivid news images. The baby boomers' collective consciousness was molded by the patchwork of TV images seen during their formative years. David Sheff, writing for *Rolling Stone*, said: "Their prime source of news was a six-inch figure named Walter Cronkite, sponsored by Pepsi and Handi-Wipes. A prime source of their values was the homilies of families called the Nelsons, the Cleavers, the Petries, the Bunkers, and the Ewings."[17]

But therein lies a paradox. Although baby boomers collectively experienced the same events through the medium of television, their reactions are anything but unified. On social, economic, political, and spiritual issues boomers are dramatically diverse.

Some (18 percent) pursued a counterculture lifestyle, whereas many others strongly opposed it. Some baby boomers are extremely affluent, but most struggle to make ends meet even with two incomes. They are volatile politically and react to a mix of issues that cannot easily be categorized as liberal or conservative. And their religious commitment is mixed. Although half said they were less involved in organized religion than they expected to be, nearly a fourth (22 percent) identified themselves as born-again Christians.[18]

But diversity is only one problem in labeling this generation, because baby boomers are forever changing. Any attempt to accurately define them as a whole would be only a snapshot of the changing views and lifestyles of a socially evolving generation. They were the Spock babies and the Sputnik generation in the 1950s, the radicals in the 1960s, the Me Generation in the 1970s, and the Yuppies or the New Collars of the 1980s.

DEFINING THE BABY BOOM

Although it is difficult to generalize about seventy-six million people, we will use two different methods of categorization to identify key segments of this generation. The first simply looks at the year of birth. (The differences will be addressed further in later chapters.) Members of the leading edge of the baby boom (born from 1946 through 1955) generally had positive experiences as they grew up. They were first to the schools, first to the universities, first to the jobs, and first to the houses. They were taught in classrooms filled with the smell of fresh paint. They attended grade schools, high schools, and colleges with little competition. When they graduated, they headed into a job market brimming with possibilities. And when it came time to buy a house, many of them purchased houses that were generally inexpensive and appreciating in value.

A GENERATION OF LABELS

SILENT GENERATION, early 1950s
First used by *Time* to describe the majority of Americans during the Eisenhower years. People content to follow prevailing rules of business. Portrayed in Sloan Wilson's *The Man in the Grey Flannel Suit*.

BEATNIKS, mid-1950s
An outgrowth of the "beat generation" described in Jack Kerouac's *On the Road*. Known for their interest in music and poetry and their rejection of jobs and social conformity.

HIPPIES, 1960s
Also known as the "flower children." Name came from a San Francisco political organization known as H.I.P. (Haight-Ashbury Independent Proprietors). Preached free love and peace.

YIPPIES, late 1960s
Members of the Youth International Party organized by Jerry Rubin and Abbie Hoffman. Known for civil disobedience and antiwar activism.

SILENT MAJORITY, 1969
First coined by Richard Nixon to describe voters he considered his backers. People "whose individual opinions are not colorful or different enough to make the news, but whose collective opinion, when crystallized, makes history."

ME GENERATION, 1976

Tom Wolfe coined this term in an article in *New York* magazine to describe boomers who put their consciences aside and plunged headlong into a quest for self-fulfillment.

PREPPIES, late 1970s

Forerunners of the yuppies. Neat, buttoned-down people with the "Ivy League" look popularized by Lisa Birnbach's 1980 book, *The Official Preppy Handbook*.

YUPPIES, 1984

Bob Greene coined this term as a 1980s update of the 1960s yippie. *Newsweek* designated 1984 as "The Year of the Yuppie." Marissa Piesman and Marilee Hartley popularized the lifestyle of the "young, upwardly mobile professional" in *The Yuppie Handbook*.

NEW COLLARS, 1985

Coined to describe the more than twenty million boomers ignored by the media but nevertheless the backbone of U.S. society with incomes between $15,000 and $30,000 a year.

Adapted from "Beatniks, Preppies and Punkers—The Love Affair with Labels," *U.S. News and World Report*, 16 September 1985, 63.

The trailing edge of the baby boom (born from 1956 through 1964) encountered a much different world. Usually they were the last to the schools, last to the universities, last to the jobs, and last to the houses. The schools they attended were often in disrepair and overcrowded, so they had less opportunity to interact with their teachers. They faced stiff competition for their college and graduate schools. When they headed out into the job market, they found that most of the jobs had been taken by their brothers and sisters in the leading edge of the boom. And many found themselves priced out of the real estate market due to increased housing prices, inflation, and lower paying jobs.

Marketers and advertisers have used another method to categorize this generation. This method of segmentation quickly kills the canard that all baby boomers are yuppies. Nothing could be further from the truth.

During the 1980s, the J. Walter Thompson agency segmented the baby boom population by plotting the two variables of education and income.[19] First, they separated the highly educated baby boomers (those with four years or more of college) from the less educated. Second, they separated the high income baby boomers (those with more than $35,000/year in personal income) from those with lower incomes. When they juxtaposed those two dimensions of education and income, they were able to identify four segments.

Two groups are already familiar. The high income, high education group is the upscale consumer that we call *yuppie*. The low income, low education group is the mass consumer that we call *worker*.

The two other groups are less familiar but also significant. The high income, low education group is called the blue collar elite, or *elite workers*. And the last group is unique in history. Because of the large number of students who got a college education in the 1960s and 1970s, and because of the competition of the baby boom generation with itself in the market, many highly educated boomers were not able to translate their academic credentials into high-paying jobs. This group has high education but low income and is called *would-be's* because they would be yuppies if they could be.

Certainly the most visible segment of the baby boom generation is the yuppies, whose influence is much greater than their numbers. Yuppies represent only about 6 percent of the baby boom population, but their numbers are expected to double during the 1990s.

Despite their acronym, a majority of yuppies are neither young nor urban. Most are now middle-aged, and half live in the suburbs. Although they were responsible for much of the gentrification of the cities, only a quarter (28 percent) of yuppies live in cities.

Yuppies have, in the past, been identified with the singles lifestyle. That is changing. More than three-fourths (77 percent) of this segment were married in the 1980s.

Yuppies are noted for their confidence and consumption. They are self-assured and confident about who they are and what they want. They are the trendsetters of this generation because they dominate the public forum and are the most vocal segment of the baby boom generation.

They are also identified with conspicuous consumption. In the past they bought the most expensive clothes and products, but those patterns may be changing, especially as they enter the years of family formation.

The second segment, the elite workers, represents about 5 percent of the baby boom population. They are the top of the

Segments of the Baby Boom

	High Income	High Income	
Low Education	Elite Workers	Yuppies	High Education
Low Education	Workers	Would-be's	High Education
	Low Income	Low Income	

working class and include repairmen, machinists, and plumbers who make more than $35,000 per year.

About 80 percent of elite workers are married. Despite their enormous purchasing power, they are largely ignored by marketers and advertisers. They are the most politically conservative and are the most likely to endorse traditional social values.

Elite workers experience a great deal of status insecurity and have reservations about themselves. Despite their affluence and income, they believe they don't have what it takes to make it in society.

The third segment, the would-be's, represent 22 percent of the baby boom population. As they enter their peak earning years, many will become yuppies, causing the yuppie population to nearly double. But the vast majority of would-be's will never become yuppies. Typical would-be's are pharmacists, teachers, managers, and social workers. They are the least conservative of the baby boom population.

The last segment is the workers, who represent two-thirds (67 percent) of this generation. The term *workers* may be deceiving here. In the past, most workers were in the manufacturing sector of the economy. Now many more are in the service sector. These are not only assembly-line or steel workers. They include cashiers, receptionists, and data-entry operators. They are the least optimistic and least satisfied with their lives. They are struggling to make ends meet and generally have little chance for improving the financial circumstances of their lives.

Each of the four segments of the baby boom generation influences the consumer market but none more than the high income segments. Although their numbers are small, the income share for yuppies and elite workers is sizable. As they reach their peak earning years, these two segments constitute the affluent market, whereas the would-be's and workers make up the mass market.

This then is a snapshot of the baby boom generation: a generation that is both unified and divided. Throughout this book, we will seek to maintain the tension between differences and similarities. In some cases, the differences in the baby boom generation are more significant than the similarities. In other cases, the similarities are more important.

NOTES

1. Paul Light, *Baby Boomers* (New York: Norton, 1988), 23.
2. Population Reference Bureau, *America's Baby Boom Generation: The Fateful Bulge* (Washington, D.C.: Population Reference Bureau, April 1980), 4.
3. Landon Jones, *Great Expectations: America and the Baby Boom Generation* (New York: Ballantine, 1980), 42.
4. Ibid., 54.
5. Benjamin Spock, *The Common Sense Book of Baby and Child Care*, 3d ed. (New York: Duell, Sloan & Pearce, 1957), 1-2. In his new introduction, Dr. Spock said: "If you are an older reader of this book, you'll see that a lot has been added and changed, especially about discipline, spoiling and the parents' part. When I was writing the first edition, between 1943 and 1946, the attitude of people toward infant feeding, toilet training, and general child management was still strict and inflexible. Since that time a great change in attitude has occurred, and nowadays there seems to be more chance of a conscientious parent's getting into trouble with permissiveness than with strictness. So I have tried to give a more balanced view."
6. Jones, *Great Expectations*, 68.
7. Ibid., 50–51.
8. Ibid., 51.
9. Quoted in Light, *Baby Boomers*, 20.
10. Jones, *Great Expectations*, 56.

11. Daniel Boorstin, "The New Barbarians," in *The Decline in Radicalism* (New York: Random, 1969).

12. Jones, *Great Expectations*, 99.

13. Marshall McLuhan, *Understanding Media: The Extensions of Man* (New York: New American, 1964).

14. William Greider, "The Rolling Stone Survey," *Rolling Stone*, 7 April 1988, 34.

15. Ibid., 36.

16. Ibid., 35.

17. David Sheff, "Portrait of a Generation," *Rolling Stone*, 5 May 1988, 46.

18. Greider, *Rolling Stone*, 34.

19. Peter Kim, "The Emergence of the 90s Consumer: Segmenting the Baby Boom," presentation at American Demographics, 1989.

CHAPTER TWO
THE HISTORY
OF THE BABY BOOM

T he baby boom generation has always believed that it is a chosen generation. Since its beginning, it has thrived in a cultural greenhouse that has cultivated its optimism, enthusiasm, and identity.

It was a generation of "great expectations." In writing about the baby boom generation, Landon Jones even borrowed that title from Charles Dickens's classic to describe one of the foundational aspects of this group. Although incredibly diverse, boomers' great expectations, more than any other psychological or sociological factor, bind them together.

But though they grew up in a time of optimism and idealism, they now live their adult lives in a world of struggle and cynicism. As a result, many face a crisis of expectations as they begin to come to grips with the crushing reality of downward mobility.

THE FORMATIVE YEARS

The 1950s and early 1960s were the formative years for baby boomers. Their expectations about lifestyles, careers, and life in general were formed in those decades. They did not experience an economic depression, a national malaise, or constrained options in personal expression in that time. On the contrary, they lived in what were atypical decades.

The 1950s and early 1960s were not just unusual decades. In hindsight, we can say confidently that they were unique. The unique aspects of those years powerfully influenced this generation as every generation is marked by its early years. First and foremost, they were years of unprecedented affluence. The postwar period and ensuing decades were not only a boom for babies—they were a boom for the economy. As the engines of war were now used to develop and build products of peace, the consumer market was filled with new appliances and conveniences.

The baby boom itself was responsible for much of that economic boom. With three million (and later four million) babies born each year, markets for baby products, clothes, houses, and so on were expanding simply because the population was expanding. The peacetime economic expansion paralleled the population expansion, causing one headline in *Life* to proclaim that the baby boom was a "built-in recession cure."[1]

Although it may be tempting to minimize and even disregard the astonishing economic growth during this period, we must not forget how unique those decades were, especially when compared to the decades that preceded and succeeded them. During that unparalleled expansion of the economy, the parents of baby boomers saw their family income double in real purchasing power.[2] Between 1947 and 1953, for example, real per capita disposable income increased by 12 percent (and this at the time when the baby boom was adding more than three million new *capita* every year).[3] Previous and later generations saw nothing even close to that.

Unlike their depression-era parents who learned to survive in the bleak times of a "fixed pie" economy, baby boomers grew up in the world of an "expanding pie" with bountiful options and great expectations. By the time the pie stopped expanding and began to shrink in the 1970s, the mind-set of boomers was fixed. They were already accustomed to living in a world of affluence and opportunities.

Second, baby boomers grew up in a time of national optimism. In a real sense, they were the generation for which World War II was fought. The nineteen-year baby boom was a reflection of that postwar optimism. Initially, demographers saw the boom

Median Family Income
in 1987 Dollars

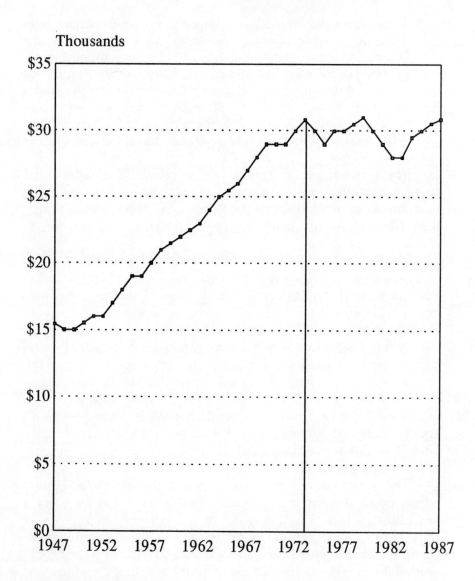

Source: U.S. Census Bureau.

as nothing more than a postwar phenomenon: postponed procreation disrupted by the war. After all, the postwar baby boom was short-lived in most countries (especially in Europe). But a few countries (all on the new frontier) experienced a prolonged period of procreation:

> These were the countries of hope, new worlds where lives could begin again. Canada, Australia, New Zealand, and the United States were all originally settled by long-distance immigrants, people who had staked their lives on the future. All four countries, further, had both rich natural resources and a frontier open for settlement. All were spacious and were considered underpopulated. All four countries had—and *still* have —the world's highest rates of individual mobility.[4]

The postwar period was a time to rebuild the nations and plot a new course for the future. Families were ready to enjoy the benefits of peace and prosperity. When confronted with a potential crisis, optimistic Americans merely rekindled their resolve to conquer the obstacle.

On October 4, 1957, the optimism of the Eisenhower years was shaken by the news that a 184-pound Russian satellite called Sputnik was orbiting the earth. But instead of allowing the revelation to dampen their spirits, Americans mustered new resolve "to beat the Russians in space."

A few years later, when a young president confidently predicted that we would put a man on the moon by the end of the decade, no one doubted. But consider the contrast between President John Kennedy's space speech and President Jimmy Carter's infamous "malaise speech," with its countless references to an energy crisis and Americans held hostage, less than two decades later. The difference poignantly illustrates how quickly this nation lost its optimism.

The erosion of our optimism began in the late 1960s. Drugs, crime, political assassinations, and the Vietnam War were but a few of the reasons. But it may not be too extreme to suggest that unrealistic expectations was a major reason this generation traded optimism for pessimism and exchanged altruism for narcissism. Baby boomers expected more from life than it could deliver, and they were led to believe they could change their world far too easily than was possible.

Differences Between Generations

	BOOMERS' GENERATION	PARENTS' GENERATION
Success oriented, place importance on getting ahead	66%	16%
Cynical about politics, distrust people in elected office	53%	29%
Place emphasis on having a close-knit family life	11%	66%
Put emphasis on organized religion and involvement in church	8%	75%
Respectful of authority, obey the rules	8%	76%
Follow traditions, believe tried-and-true methods are best	8%	77%

Boomers were asked: "Do you think each of the following items better describes your generation or your parents' generation?" Reported in David Sheff, "What Really Matters," *Rolling Stone*, May 5, 1988, 53.

While we were still living in the age of optimism, the editors of *Time* chose the under-twenty-five generation as their "Man of the Year." Still enchanted by the promise of this chosen generation, the editors delivered this amazing prophecy: "Untold adventure awaits him. He is the man who will land on the moon, cure cancer and the common cold, lay out blight-proof, smog-free cities, enrich the underdeveloped world and, no doubt, write finis to poverty and war."[5]

No wonder baby boomers were slowly being crushed under the weight of such expectations. When this "can-do" generation met the harsh realities of life, it discovered that intractable problems such as ecology, poverty, and war weren't to be solved as easily as they had been led to believe.

The optimism of those formative years had a profound impact on boomers' worldview. It, no doubt, was another reason for the oft-discussed "generation gap." Members of the Depression-era generation saw life as hard, where toil and struggle created opportunity. For them (to borrow another phrase from Charles Dickens) it was the best of times and it was the worst of times. They enjoyed the freedom and opportunity the country provided, but they worked long and hard to achieve the American dream.

By contrast, baby boomers grew up in a world ripe for the plucking. They lived in a time of extraordinary national optimism, idealism, and economic expansion. Often they were indulged, both materially and emotionally, by their newly affluent parents and by the society that surrounded them. Their world built new schools for them, invented new products for them, and took its cultural cues from them.

That unique set of circumstances molded in the minds of most boomers an attitude that Daniel Yankelovich has called "the psychology of entitlement."[6] This generation began to believe that it was entitled to the best things life could offer. What other generations viewed as privileges, baby boomers believed were rights.

The predictable result was disillusionment. A generation growing up in that unusual period of affluence, optimism, and opportunity expected more from life than it could possibly deliver. In his book *Great Expectations*, Landon Jones put it this way:

> The baby boomers' idea of an appropriate living standard was fixed, for many of them, on the living standards of the 1950s and early 1960s. In retrospect I think this was dangerous to their psychological welfare. The most atypical American decade was not the turbulent sixties, which were not all that different from, say, the thirties or even twenties. Rather, the truly atypical American decade was the fifties, with its extraordinary tranquillity and prosperity.[7]

A third factor influencing baby boomers was the expectations of their parents. This generation was reared to believe that it was *special*. They were born in the postwar wonder years to parents who instilled in them a sense of destiny.

Depression-era parents deprived of many of the necessities of life determined to provide the best that life could offer to their children. Hard work, sacrifice, and rising affluence made it possible for parents in the 1950s and 1960s to give their children the toys, cars, and education they had been denied.

Here again a generation gap was created. Whereas the parents of baby boomers saw a teenager who owned a car or went to college as uniquely privileged, most of their children took such things for granted and viewed them as their birthright.[8]

Depression-era parents also decided to give their children the time and attention they had often been denied in their youth. Reinforcing that view was the ever-present manual by Dr. Benjamin Spock that rejected the Victorian values of regimented schedules. Dr. Spock's philosophy allowed and even encouraged a degree of parental indulgence.

The message that boomers were special was further reinforced by a technological innovation that set them apart: the television set. They were the first "TV generation" and thus perceived the world and themselves in ways distinct from any previous generation.

When the boom began, only a few thousand television sets existed. By the early 1950s, more than ten million sets were already in use. When the fifties came to an end, more than four out of every five households had at least one TV set, and by the mid-1960s, 98 percent of all homes had sets.[9]

Television set this generation apart from all others. Social commentators have discussed and documented at length on the wide and varied impact the medium has had on generations reared in its ubiquitous glow. Some of the consequences that are relevant here are increased expectations, heightened social awareness, and decreased family time it fostered. Television became not merely a window to the world but a constant companion and electronic baby-sitter.

Most of all, television reinforced the notion that this generation was indeed *special*. It was as if the world invented TV just for them: to inform, to entertain, and most of all to sell the products and services boomers quickly learned to crave.

Indulged at nearly every turn, people in this generation inevitably developed unrealistic and unhealthy expectations. The lessons they learned came not from parents, but from television and their own youth culture. They rejected their parents' values of hard work and self-sacrifice, believing that prosperity and opportunity were their birthright. Instead of self-sacrifice, they sought self-expression which, along with personal freedom, became the cornerstone of their lifestyles. Self-fulfillment became their greatest ambition.

Unfortunately, the generation convinced it has a special place in history has not been very successful in finding that place. Its great dreams and aspirations have been shattered frequently by the harsh realities of life.

UNFULFILLED EXPECTATIONS

When those of the baby boom generation hit the late 1960s and 1970s, they experienced a collective crisis of expectations as they began their careers. The crisis continued as they began to look for housing and start families. As we will discuss in a subsequent chapter, that inability to achieve the American dream will further intensify into a full-blown crisis of disillusionment.

The career crisis was due to two factors: size and timing. When the first baby boomers graduated from high school in the mid-1960s, they set in motion a trend not unlike that previously experienced in the schools a few years before. The pig was continuing to move through the python, creating an inevitable job squeeze. Put simply, Americans had made babies faster in the 1940s and 1950s than the economy could make jobs for them in the 1960s and 1970s. Before boomers entered the job market, the number of twenty-five-to-thirty-four-year-old workers oscillated between fourteen and seventeen million. But as boomers began to start careers, that number exploded from seventeen million in 1970 to more than thirty million by 1985.[10]

The impact on the boom generation was devastating, especially for college graduates who assumed that their diplomas would quickly translate into good jobs and quick promotions. "For the first time in American history, the relative earnings of college graduates *declined*. As an investment, college was costing more but was worth less."[11]

Unfortunately, the best educated generation was also the largest, and therefore its members found themselves competing with each other for jobs and advancements. Each graduating class poured more applicants into an already tight job market. Some found entry-level jobs in their career. But a larger number had to settle for jobs substantially beneath their academic preparation. It was not uncommon in the 1970s to find out that your waiter had a Ph.D. in sociology or that your taxi driver was finishing a master's degree in English. Overtrained graduates found themselves underemployed, if not unemployed, because of the surplus of applicants.

The second factor affecting the career crisis was timing. Their vast numbers had a significant effect on their ability to find work, but the timing of their entry into the job market could not have been worse. The boom in the economy paralleled and even exceeded the boom in births. But by the early 1970s economic expansion had stopped and begun to decline.

> From the end of World War II through 1973, real wages in the U.S. had grown at an average of almost 3 percent per year. The age growth reflected rapid gains in worker productivity and it permitted routine pay increases above specific career paths. During these years, an average man passing from age 40 to 50 would see his real earnings rise by 25 to 30 percent even though his big promotions were behind him. . . . This wage growth was the norm through 1973. Then it stopped. A man aged 40 in 1973 would be lucky to be earning as much today as he did then.[12]

Why such a precipitous decline? Not all the reasons are clear, but some can be listed. One reason was the increase in OPEC oil prices. The oil price hikes in 1973-74 and 1979-80 lowered the purchasing power of wages by about 5 percent.

A second reason was a decline in worker productivity. During the years of the baby boom (specifically 1947 to 1965), productivity in the private sector increased by an annual average of 3.3 percent. Graduates in the early 1970s were accustomed to the productivity, prosperity, and opportunity of the 1950s. And what productivity! In 1953, for example, a nation that had only 7 percent of the world's population produced two-thirds of its manufactured products, owned three-quarters of its cars and appliances, and purchased 33 percent of all the goods and services available on the planet.[13] Between 1965 and 1972, however, productivity decreased to 2.4 percent a year and slipped further to 1.6 percent for most of the 1970s.[14] The boom generation hardly knew what hit it.

The sheer numbers of this generation were sufficient to limit job selection and stifle career advancement. And baby boomers had the added misfortune of starting their careers just as economic productivity ran out of gas, both literally and figuratively.

A generation reared to feel it was entitled to upward mobility began to face the very real prospects of *downward* mobility. Although boomers saw their parents succeed and advance in their careers, their own prospects did not appear so rosy.

Notice the following trend in wage increases for men. (We will discuss women's wages and impact on the work force in the next chapter.) The typical thirty-year-old working man in 1949 saw his median income swell by 63 percent by the time he reached age forty. By comparison, a thirty-year-old man in 1959 would see his median income increase 49 percent by age forty. But by the 1970s, the trend was no longer upward but slightly downward. A thirty-year-old in 1973 found that by the time he was forty, his earnings had actually declined by a percent.[15]

That decline affected the mind-set not only of those in the job market but of students still in college. Faced with what appeared to be a deteriorating economy, college students began to rethink their priorities and their majors. Surveys done by the American Council of Education between 1968 and 1972 showed that about 50 percent of male freshmen believed that "being very well off financially" was essential or very important. By the fall of 1973, when the economy turned sour, that number had increased to 62 percent, and it reached 69 percent by the end of the decade.[16] The lesson was not lost on the generation following the boomers. By 1987, that proportion reached 76 percent.[17]

An even more dramatic contrast of values surfaces when we compare the 1967 survey with the 1987 survey. In 1967, 44 percent felt that "being well off financially" was important, whereas 83 percent of those interviewed thought it crucial "to develop a philosophy of life." Twenty years later, those percentages had reversed. Financial security was important to 76 percent, whereas a philosophy of life was important only to 39 percent.[18]

Unlike the generation that preceded them, members of the boom generation faced intra-generational competition and economic stagnation and wound up with fewer jobs, fewer promotions, and lower wages than previous generations. Not only did those factors put them at a disadvantage in the job market; they also affected their ability to participate in the housing market and in society in general.

HOPE IN THE MIDST OF BROKEN PROMISES

To a generation reared on the American dream, the shock of the tight job market (as well as other difficulties) should have generated a crisis of expectations. For most boomers, however, it did not. The reasons are due to demographics and denial.

First, these crises did not affect boomers uniformly. Both age and race were relevant factors. The leading edge of the boom generation again had the advantage over younger boomers. They were the first to the grade schools in the fifties, first to the colleges in the sixties, and first to the jobs in the seventies. Thus, they were able to realize many more of their expectations than the trailing edge.

Boomers at the back of the pack hit a job market that was already crowded by their older brothers and sisters. They had fewer job choices, often at lower wages. They also saw little opportunity for career advancement since the upper echelons were often crowded with boomers who had joined the company five to ten years earlier. They are now beginning to fear that they will completely miss out on the American dream.

In addition to age, race was another factor that determined who suffered the crises most severely. Whereas white unemployment was disturbing, black unemployment was devastating. Among black youths, unemployment experienced a nearly twelvefold increase from 3.4 percent in 1955 to just under 40 percent in 1980. Moreover, the unemployment rate for black teenagers was twice that of white teenagers—and the gap is widening.[19] In nearly every statistic we will consider in this book, the forces affecting boomers in general were magnified against blacks and most other minority races.

But whether young or old, black or white, millions in this generation experienced the regret of unfulfilled expectations. One writer expressed her feelings of downward mobility this way:

> Not long after we married, my husband and I flew to Connecticut to visit my parents. We carried our second-hand suitcases up to what was once my brother's bedroom. The room was richer than I remembered. The bed had a real box spring; a cashmere blanket lay folded at its base.
>
> Outside the window, rain from a sprinkler fell on a long lawn sloping into the trees. Every room in my parents' house whispered of surplus space and money and time. I took off my shoes and thought to myself, "I will never live this way again."[20]

Surprisingly, though, many members of this generation express a degree of hope in the midst of the disturbing trends.

Whether it is denial, latent optimism, or a lack of understanding of their situation, a majority of baby boomers are still fairly optimistic about their careers and prospects for the future. Nearly half said they were extremely satisfied with their jobs, and 63 percent were also extremely satisfied with their prospects of getting ahead in the future.[21]

Yet such optimism about the future does not transfer to present economic circumstances. On the surface boomers appear optimistic, but beneath the surface there is growing anxiety. Only 31 percent felt satisfied that they were financially secure, and 17 percent were extremely dissatisfied with their economic situation.[22]

A more telling statistic is how baby boomers describe their own incomes. Unlike the media stereotype, most baby boomers are not affluent, free-spending yuppies who drive BMWs. One survey of the baby boom generation found that the median household income was $28,000. When the same baby boomers were asked what income they needed in order to live without money worries, they said $38,500.[23] At the moment, at least, this generation is living substantially below its economic expectations and anticipated needs.

When boomers were asked to compare their standard of living to their parents, the age differential of this generation surfaced. Three-fourths of older boomer men and two-thirds of older boomer women believe their present standard of living is better than their parents during the last years they lived at home. By contrast, only half of young boomer men and women thought their circumstances were better than their parents.[24]

Many are facing the reality that they have to work harder and have fewer opportunities than their parents. Forty-eight percent, for example, think it is more difficult to earn a comfortable living now than when their parents were their age.[25] Reinforcing that notion was a report issued by the Joint Economic Committee in the mid-1980s concluding that young adults were not able to achieve a standard of living comparable to their parents.[26]

The baby boom generation began with great expectations, but it has encountered some unexpected potholes on the road to success. As baby boomers make their way toward the twenty-first century, they must come to grips with the changing economic circumstances of society. But society must also make room for the changing social circumstances of the boom generation as boomers form families.

NOTES

1. "Kids: Built-in Recession Cure—How 4,000,000 a Year Make Millions in Business," *Life*, 16 June 1958.
2. Cited in Landon Jones, *Great Expectations: America and the Baby Boom Generation* (New York: Ballantine, 1980), 3.
3. Figures taken from a series of articles in Fortune on "The Changing American Market." Found in Laurence Shames, *The Hunger for More* (New York: Times Books, 1989), 55.
4. Jones, *Great Expectations*, 23.
5. "Man of the Year: Twenty-five and Under," *Time*, 6 January 1967, 18.
6. Jones, *Great Expectations*, 300.
7. Ibid., 5.
8. One statistical example is the difference in the number who attended college. "While only one out of every ten Americans born in 1905 had any college training, one in every three born in 1955 has been to college." Cited in Jones, *Great Expectations*, 100.
9. Since 1967, approximately 97-98 percent of American homes have TV sets. In fact, more American homes have TV sets than have indoor plumbing (George Gerbner, "Living with Television," *Journal of Communication*, Spring 1976, 175).
10. Frank Levy and Richard Michel, "Are Baby Boomers Selfish?" *American Demographics*, April 1985, 38.
11. Jones, *Great Expectations*, 179.
12. Levy and Michel, "Are Baby Boomers Selfish?" 38–39.
13. "Business in 1953—A Keystone of the Free World," *Time*, 4 January 1954, 54ff.
14. The Council of Economic Advisers, Economic Report of the President, February 1984.
15. "The Average Guy Takes It on the Chin," *New York Times*, 13 July 1986, section 3.
16. Levy and Michel, "Are Baby Boomers Selfish?" 40.
17. Shames, *The Hunger for More*, 43.
18. Ibid.
19. Jones, *Great Expectations*, 188.
20. Katy Butler, "Lowered Expectations: A Baby Boomer Comes to Terms with an Era of Downward Mobility," *Dallas Morning News*, 9 July 1989, 4.
21. William Greider, "Money Matters," *Rolling Stone*, 7 April 1988, 47.
22. Ibid.
23. Ibid.
24. Fabian Linden, "The Dream Is Alive," *American Demographics*, June 1986, 4.
25. Greider, "Money Matters," 47.
26. Frank S. Levy and Richard C. Michel, "The Economic Future of the Baby Boom," Joint Economic Committee, U.S. Congress, 22 November 1985.

CHAPTER THREE
THE FAMILIES
OF THE BABY BOOM

T he family is the foundation of society. It is the most basic social institution, and the future of any culture rests upon the strength of the families that compose it. But in recent decades, what has come to be called the "traditional family" has undergone profound alterations. Baby boomers reared in traditional families in the 1950s are venturing out in the 1990s into the uncharted territory of nontraditional families.

Some of the changes in family structure can be attributed to changing social and psychological attitudes, such as materialism and narcissism. And although that is certainly the case (and will be discussed in a later chapter), the driving force behind these changes was changing economic conditions in the 1970s.

ECONOMIC FORCES ON FAMILY FORMATION

As we have noted, the boom generation faced a career crisis due to both size and timing. The size of the generation substantially increased the supply of applicants beyond demand. Declines in worker productivity and OPEC oil price shocks exacerbated the situation. Thus, the boom generation ended up with fewer jobs, fewer promotions, lower salaries, and fewer pay raises than previous generations.

Although those economic factors affected everyone, they hit the boom generation hardest for two reasons. First is the issue of pecking order. When the labor market is in the midst of transition and has to make sudden adjustments, the last on the scene usually bear the greatest costs. "An employer might have trouble denying a cost-of-living adjustment to a long-time employee, but it was easy to let inflation erode starting salaries. This made it particularly hard for baby boomers to get a decent foothold."[1]

Second, the boom generation was beginning to start families and therefore was in the market for houses. Older workers, who had purchased homes before the seventies began, benefited by the economic conditions. They had purchased their homes at low prices with low-interest loans. During the 1970s, they could pay off their mortgages with increasingly inflated dollars as they watched the values of their homes substantially appreciate.

Not so for people in the boom generation. They were just starting their families and entering the housing market. Consider this father-son comparison:

> Suppose a young man of 18 or 19 was preparing to leave his parents' home. As he left, he saw what his father's salary would buy and he kept the memory as a personal yardstick. In the 1950s or 1960s, the young man would have quickly measured up. By age 30, he already would have been earning one-third more than his father earned when the young man left home. But today a 30-year-old man is earning about 10 percent less than his father earned when he left home.[2]

Boomers facing downward mobility during what had traditionally been the peak years for family formation faced a dilemma. Raising a family usually requires increasing consumption: buying a house, buying baby clothes, buying another car, and so on. In order to make that possible, the boom generation made adjustments. And these three adjustments explain, in large part, why families in the 1990s are so different from families in the 1950s.

First, boomers postponed marriage. They waited until after they had established their careers to get married. Since 1973, the median age of first marriages increased by nearly two years for women and more than two years for men. Those figures have, in fact, reached the highest levels since the turn of the century.

Household Income
By Age of Head of Household

Average household income (Thousands)

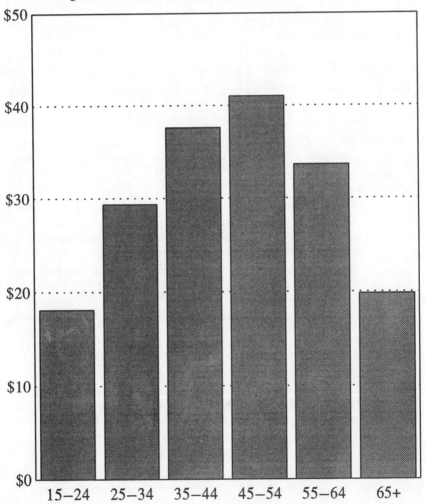

Source: U.S. Census Bureau.

One Wage Earner
Versus Two Wage Earner

	NEED TWO FULL-TIME WAGE EARNERS	COMFORTABLE WITH ONE FULL-TIME WAGE EARNER
All Respondents	48%	31%
Single	47%	31%
Traditional Marriage*	25%	53%
Modern Marriage**	62%	20%
Divorced or Widowed with Children	44%	30%

* "Traditional marriage" describes respondents who said they were married and had never been divorced, who indicated that only the husband worked, and who had children.

** "Modern marriage" describes respondents who said they were married and had never been divorced but who indicated that both husband and wife worked.

Source: Respondents were asked, "Some people say that to make a comfortable living, a family must have two full-time wage earners. Do you agree with this, or do you think a family can make a comfortable living with only one full-time wage earner?" Reported in William Greider, "Money Matters," *Rolling Stone*, May 5, 1988, 48.

Second, both husband and wife went to work. The traditional family structure of a breadwinner husband and a homemaker wife was replaced by dual income couples, spawning such acronyms as "dinks"—double income, no kids. Boomers who postponed marriage did not substantially change their career plans once they got married. Among twenty-five-to-thirty-four-year-old married couples, 47 percent of the wives worked in 1973. By 1985, the percentage had already grown to 65 percent[3] and is continuing to increase.

Third, they postponed procreation. Unlike their parents, boomers waited longer to get married and longer to have children. And once they had children, they had fewer of them. Children, though a blessing, have become increasingly expensive to rear. Parents of a baby born in 1979 could expect to pay $66,000 to rear the child to age eighteen. For a baby born in 1988, parents could expect to pay $150,000, and that did not include the additional costs of piano lessons, summer camp, or a college education.[4]

The combined effect of those three adjustments was dramatic. Nationally, per capita consumption rose in the 1970s in a way reminiscent of the 1950s. But the difference is instructive. In the 1950s, the labor pool was constant (at about 40 percent) while wages rose. In the 1970s, wages were relatively constant, so the increase in per capita consumption rose because the labor force itself increased.[5]

BABY BOOM FAMILIES

Although most baby boomers have constructed families different from the ones of their youth, still lingering in their memories is an image of what the family is supposed to be like. For most, the concept of the traditional family was fixed in their minds during the 1950s. That ideal included a breadwinning father and a homemaking mother. Such parents presumably were in their first marriage and focused most of their time and energy on their children.

That image was reinforced at every turn. Television, for example, reinforced the stereotype with shows such as "Donna Reed," "Ozzie and Harriet," and "Leave it to Beaver." They portrayed families in which the father went off to work (even though Ozzie Nelson seemed to hang around the house most of the time) and the mother stayed home to keep house and rear the children. Although it was a television stereotype, it was a generally accurate image of families during that period. Seventy percent of households in the 1950s and 60 percent of households in the 1960s were composed of a working man, a nonworking wife, and one or more children under eighteen.[6]

But that image of the traditional family has been substantially redefined during the lifetime of most baby boomers. Changing economic, as well as social, conditions have transformed the status of the traditional family from a majority to a dwindling minority. By the start of the 1980s, only 14 percent of families fit that category, and by the beginning of the 1990s they represented only 7 percent of American households.[7]

Changing Families
Composition of U.S. Households

Other families
11%

Living alone
15%

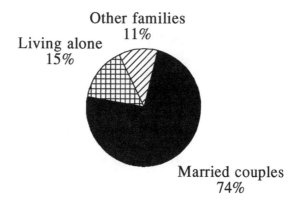

Married couples
74%

1960

Living alone
32%

Other families
15%

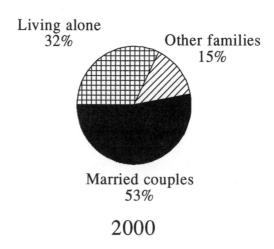

Married couples
53%

2000

Source: U.S. Census Bureau.

Instead of conforming to one ideal or model, the American family is quickly evolving into diverse entities driven by shifting morality and values. One writer said, "The New American Family is the combined family, a montage of bits and pieces from other families now joined in holy pandemonium."[8]

Given current trends, some experts suggest that even references to "the family" may become obsolete. Psychologist Fitzhugh Dodson said, "There will be no one family of the future; there will be many families."[9] Just as there has been a pluralization of philosophies and ideologies in the latter half of the twentieth century, so there has also been a pluralization of our ideas of family. In a few short decades, America has moved from extended families to nuclear families to a plurality of family structures.

The diversification of family structures occurred when baby boomers were in the midst of household formation. Although they carried with them the images of Jim and Margaret Anderson or Ward and June Cleaver, they constructed families very different from the ones of the 1950s. Families today differ from the families of the 1950s in three significant ways.

First, a high percentage of families in the 1990s are dual income families. Boomer women entered the work force in record numbers and stayed in the work force after they married. Thus, in the typical household today both the husband and the wife are employed.

The second difference is that families today are smaller. Due to economic conditions and lifestyle choices, the boom generation not only postponed marriage but postponed childbearing. When boomers began to have children, they had fewer children and thus generally have smaller families than their parents.

Third, there has been the growth of the nontraditional family household, or what the Census Bureau has defined as nonfamily households. That includes such categories as adults living alone, as well as people living together who are not related by blood or marriage.

DUAL INCOME HOUSEHOLDS

A driving force in the evolution of the family has been the dramatic increase in the number of women in the work force. Since the munitions assembly lines in World War II, women have been in the workplace. But their number has increased significantly, especially for mothers who used to postpone careers until their children were grown. Three out of every five new workers since 1947 have been women.[10]

The increase in working women is due primarily to boomer women. More than two out of every three women in the baby boom generation are currently in the labor force.[11] Thus, in a single generation they changed the typical environment of the American woman from the homefront to the workplace.

As we have stated previously, the transition occurred in the 1970s. The first landmark was the changing ratio between working women and homemakers. In previous decades, homemakers outnumbered working women. By 1972, however, the number of working women surpassed the number of housewives. The second landmark occurred in June 1978. By then, the proportion of women in the work force (aged sixteen and over) passed the 50 percent level.[12]

Boomer women not only changed the percentage in the work force; they also changed the life patterns of women. Nearly a majority of mothers of the boom generation stayed out of work to have children. And when they did go to work, they did so after they had reared their children. Boomer women changed both of those patterns. They entered the work force early and stayed longer. When they had children, they did not wait until their children were grown to return to work. A sizable number went back to work while they still had preschool children. In fact, the percentage of women with preschool children in the work force is higher than the percentage of women in the work force. The percentage of all women (aged sixteen to sixty-eight) in the work force is 56 percent and will most likely rise to 65 percent by the year 2000. When we compare that to women with preschool children (under the age of six), we find that 68 percent are already in the work force and that number will probably rise to 90 percent by the year 2000.[13]

Why did so many boomer women go to work? The reasons are numerous, but at least three significant issues should be mentioned: opportunity, ideology, and need. In agricultural societies, families were the productive unit. Women were essential to such home-based economies and rarely worked outside of the home. Women who did enter the workplace in pre-industrial America were unmarried women working in traditional gender-based occupations such as teachers, nurses, maids, clerks, dressmakers, hairdressers, librarians, and secretaries.

Fewer Families
Married Couples with Children

Percent of U.S. Households

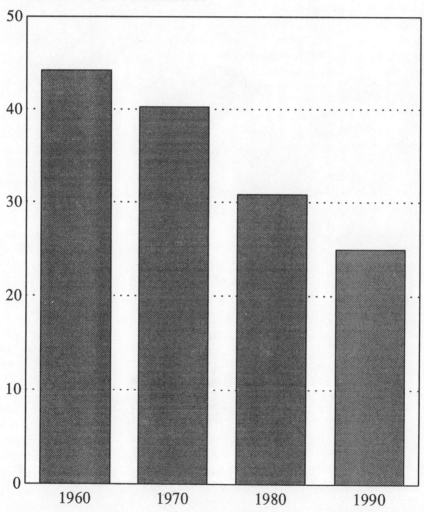

Source: U.S. Census Bureau.

Women in the Work Force

1940 total:
27.4% of women
in the work force

Widowed/divorced 15.1%

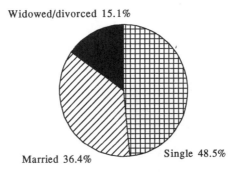

Married 36.4%   Single 48.5%

1987 total:
56% of women
in the work force

Widowed/Divorced 19.4%   Single 25.9%

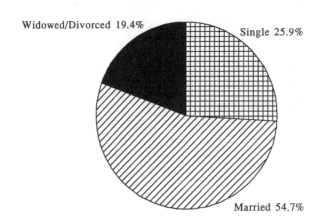

Married 54.7%

Source: U.S. Census Bureau.

During World War II, many women entered the work force to help the war effort. One icon in American history is the image of Rosie the Riveter with her sleeves rolled up and hair tucked underneath her cap. But women entered more than just the assembly lines. They took jobs at every level of the work force; for example, 38 percent of federal office workers were women. By the end of the war, twenty million women were in the labor force.[14]

After the war, America began changing from a manufacturing economy to a service economy. That provided unprecedented opportunities for women. Most of the fields with expanding opportunities (teaching and real estate, for example) already had high proportions of women. The demand for workers quickly outstripped the supply.

The baby boom increased the need for teachers and houses, but the supply of young single women was exhausted. So older, married women were drawn into the work force by the economic opportunities awaiting them.

The irony is significant. The women's revolution in the workplace was started by mothers of baby boomers who were supposedly dedicated to homemaking rather than careers. They took advantage of the changing opportunity and soon were encouraged by a changing ideology.

Betty Friedan wrote *The Feminine Mystique* in 1963. She argued that a woman could not gain ego satisfaction merely by living vicariously through her husband and children. Technological advances had diminished much of the challenge of caring for a home and so, argued Friedan, the modern woman needed a life of her own.[15] For many women that meant a career of her own.

Although such feminist ideas found little fertile soil with the older generation, they firmly took root with baby boom women who began entering the work force two years later. After 1965, a flood tide of baby boom women hit the work force. Not only were there lots of women in the baby boom, but a high percentage of them wanted to work.

Consider these statistics of women under twenty-five in the work force. Less than half of the previous generation of women (those born in the 1930s) worked in their early twenties. But when the leading edge of the baby boom generation hit, the proportion jumped to 58 percent. And by the time the trailing edge of the boom generation reached that age in 1980, the percentage was already at 69 percent.[16]

The trend also continued for later ages. Between 1960 and 1979, the proportion of young women (ages twenty-five to thirty-four) working increased from 36 percent to 64 percent.[17]

A final factor that influenced the increased number of women in the work force was economic need. The economic climate, as we have noted, was stagnant when most of the boom generation began its careers. Faced with a career crisis and a housing crisis, boomer women stayed in the work force even after they got married.

Young adults born during the baby boom found themselves caught in an unfamiliar squeeze. Between 1949 and 1973, income for families with two children doubled. After 1973, family income declined.[18]

Boomers' parents, who had started families in the 1950s, quickly exceeded the living standards of their own homes. Baby boomers starting families in the 1970s and 1980s did not do as well. They faced *downward* mobility and found it difficult to make ends meet. The solution seemed simple: send Mom back to work.

At first, husbands sent their wives to work reluctantly, but, in just over a decade, that reluctance changed. Men were asked this question: Would you prefer that your wife worked outside the home? In 1978, a plurality of men were *against* their wives working outside the home. By 1989, however, a plurality of men polled said they would *prefer* their wives to work.[19]

The implications of dual income families are many, but three are especially significant. First, the change altered our views on child rearing. A major issue, for example, of the 1990s has become day care. The two Ds of dual income and day care are inextricably entwined. Political parties and platforms cannot ignore the issue. Discussions on Capitol Hill are rarely about whether we should have a federally funded day-care system. The only significant discussion is whether to accept one party's day-care proposal over the other. The reason is simple. Women are looking for inexpensive day care and demanding it from their elected representatives.

A second implication of wives working is time. The boom generation has too many choices and too little time. Whereas the big issue in the 1980s was discretionary income, the burning issue in the 1990s is discretionary *time*. All families, but especially dual income families, face a time crunch today.

Third, the number of boom women in the work force changed not only the workplace but also the home. By going to

Wives Who Work

Percent of Married Couples

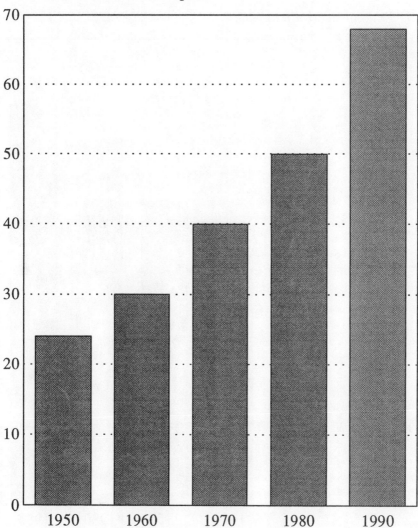

Source: U.S. Census Bureau.

Working Mothers
with Children under Six

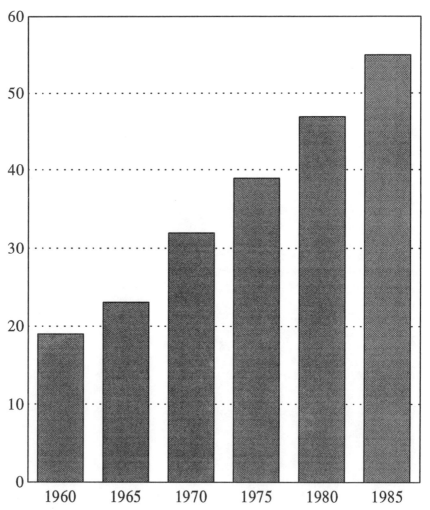

Percent of Mothers

Source: U.S. Department of Commerce.

work in record numbers, the boom generation became the last generation to be raised by homemakers.

SMALLER FAMILIES

Reversing the trend of their parents, baby boomers postponed childbearing and then ended up having fewer children and thus smaller families. The replacement rate for society is approximately 2.1 children for every woman. Already we have fallen below that replacement value with an average of about 1.8 children per woman. As Ben Wattenberg shows in his book *The Birth Dearth*, the long-term trajectory is toward a decline of the American population in the twenty-first century.[20] That will create financial concerns, which we will discuss in the chapter on a crisis in security.

When we factor in such considerations as infertility and decisions to remain childless, we see a further decline. The percentage of married households with children is dropping significantly. In 1970, 40 percent of households fit the category of "married with children." By 1987, that percentage had dropped to 27 percent.[21]

Again, the boom generation broke from its parents' attitudes and in so doing clearly defined its endpoint as a generation. Demographers had assumed that the baby boom would be followed by a baby boom echo.[22] Instead, the boom was followed by a baby bust. The leading edge (born in 1946 and after) could have kept the boom going just as the trailing edge was being born in 1964. Instead, older boomers threw out their parents' procreation ethic and postponed both marriage and childbearing.

The baby boom and the baby bust were a consequence of surprising uniformity in both timing and numbers—the bust a result of the reverse of the trends that created the boom. The timing of births in the 1950s created a bunching effect. Like an accordion being squeezed, more births occurred in those years because older women were having babies later and younger women were having babies earlier. The boom generation reversed that trend. Now the accordion was expanding, and births were thinning out over the late 1960s and 1970s.[23]

The number of children per boomer family was also very different from that of boomers' parents. During the rising affluence and optimism of the 1950s, additional children in a family were not seen as a financial burden and were essentially encouraged by the dynamism of the American dream.

Cost of Raising Children

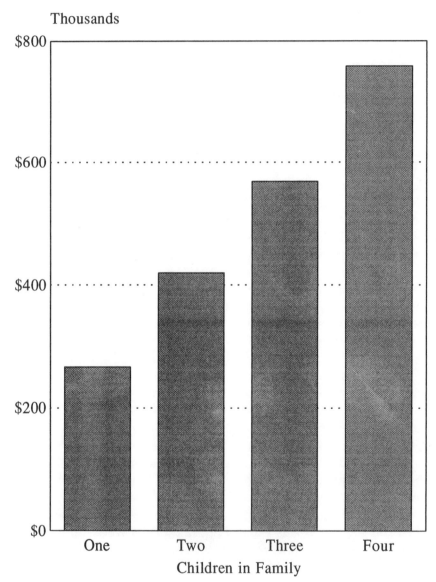

Source: U.S. Department of Agriculture.

By contrast, the boom generation was much more reticent about childbearing. An overcrowded generation accustomed to standing in line at nearly every event questioned the wisdom of adding too quickly to the human race. Further fueling that attitude were books such as Paul Ehrlich's *The Population Bomb,* along with buttons that admonished others to "Stop at Two" and bumper stickers that declared that "Jesus Was An Only Child." Simply put, childbearing in the 1950s was nearly a patriotic duty. Less than two decades later, not having children was seen as an economic and ecological responsibility.

When the decision to have fewer children was coupled with the decision to postpone childbearing, fertility rates dropped to an all-time low in the mid-1970s. Between 1960 and 1979, the percentage of married women in their early twenties who had not yet had a baby nearly doubled.[24]

Some have argued that the baby bust was merely the byproduct of the pill and abortion. But that is not the case. The decline in fertility represents a change in attitudes and was already taking place before the birth control pill was readily available and before the Supreme Court legalized abortion in its 1973 *Roe v. Wade* case. Both the pill and abortion significantly contributed to the decline, but they did not cause it.

Boom women chose not to follow their mothers into motherhood, at least not immediately. They had professional opportunities in the workplace and quickly found that they preferred paychecks to pregnancies. Moreover, they and their husbands had financial obligations that substantially raised the stakes of leaving the work force and starting a family. And unlike any generation preceding them, boomer women now had the technological means to plan both the timing and the number of their babies.

An important social implication of smaller families is that the focus has now moved from youth to adults. The fifties and sixties saw a youth-oriented culture arise simply because there were so many. But now that the pig in the python has moved on to its next life stage, the nineties have become an adult-oriented culture.

One indicator of that cultural shift can be seen on television. In the 1950s, parents could sit their children down in front of TV shows such as "Donna Reed," "Leave It to Beaver," "Ed Sullivan," and "Bonanza" and be assured that the programs would be appropriate family fare. Now, programs even during so-called "family hour" often deal with adult themes and use pictures and language that would have been considered objectionable less than two decades ago.

This shift from a child-oriented society to an adult-oriented culture occurred in large measure due to demographics. There are simply more adults than there are children. Broadcasters, programmers, and advertisers trying to reach the largest audience targeted the boom generation as youth, and today target them as adults.

But the shift also occurred because this generation of adults insists on receiving more attention than previous generations demanded. Pollster Daniel Yankelovich identified a group of parents in the late 1970s as "the New Breed." This group, composed almost entirely of baby boomers, was less child-oriented and more self-oriented. Although their parents made great sacrifices for them, nearly half of the "New Breed" agreed with this statement: "Parents should *not* sacrifice in order to give their children the best."[25]

Neil Postman, writing on *The Disappearance of Childhood*, contends that two trends are simultaneously crossing. The first is the rise of the "adultified" child. Children must grow up faster in this world and confront issues never faced by previous generations of young people, such as drugs and sexually transmitted diseases. The second trend is what Postman calls the rise of the "childified" adult. Boomer parents seem reluctant to accept their full responsibility as adults. They are less committed to meeting the needs of their children and more committed to meeting their own needs. Simply put, "American adults want to be parents of children less than they want to be children themselves."[26] Thus, we have a culture that focuses more attention on adults than it does on children.

NONTRADITIONAL HOUSEHOLDS

The Census Bureau makes a distinction between family households (where people are related to one another) and nonfamily households. As we have already noted, the traditional family is on the decline, and the nontraditional family is on the increase. Much of that increase has been documented in the Census Bureau category of nonfamily households. That includes adults living alone as well as unrelated people living together.

The number of adults living alone in the 1950s was less than 10 percent. That percentage represented a disproportionate number of widows and widowers. Today, due to death, divorce, and deferred marriage, that number is nearly a quarter of all American households.[27]

The number of adults living together has also increased. Although it is difficult to get an accurate figure, demographers estimate that there are at least two million cohabiting couples.[28]

The isolation and low level of commitment in nonfamily households will likely lead to a crisis of loneliness, which we will discuss in a later chapter. Relevant here, however, is how the sociological changes have affected our perception of the family. The editors of *Newsweek* put out a special edition dedicated to "The 21st Century Family." In an article asking the question, "What Happened to the Family?" the writer said:

> The American family does not exist. Rather, we are creating many American families, of diverse style and shapes. In unprecedented numbers, our families are unalike: we have fathers working while mothers keep house; fathers and mothers both working away from the home; single parents; second marriages bringing children together from unrelated backgrounds; childless couples; unmarried couples, with and without children; gay and lesbian parents.[29]

Certainly the demographics of the American family are changing in the 1990s.

Not only are traditional families different in terms of demographics; they are also different in their psychographics. Many have boldly proclaimed the return to traditional family values. Yet the available statistics suggest that today's families are different not only in terms of their structure but also in terms of their psychology.

Back in 1924, Helen and Robert Lynd conducted the famous "Middletown" research. During the 1920s, the Lynds asked mothers in "Middletown" (later revealed to be Muncie, Indiana) which traits they most emphasized in rearing their children. They reviewed a list of qualities and selected the following three: loyalty to the church, strict obedience, and good manners. The qualities they rated the lowest were: independence, tolerance, and social-mindedness.

In 1978, a number of sociologists returned to Muncie to survey a new generation of mothers. When they asked the same question, they selected the following three choices as the most positive traits: independence, tolerance, and social-mindedness.

The qualities they rated lowest were: good manners, loyalty to the church, and strict obedience.[30]

The survey in 1978 completely reversed the 1924 survey. In the 1920s, mothers showed a strong preference for conformity. More than a half century later, a generation of baby boom mothers had diametrically different childrearing goals. They opted instead for traits that were linked to autonomy.

The metamorphosis documented in the "Middletown" survey is not unique but has been replicated in other studies. Today's family is different from yesterday's family in terms of demographics and psychographics.

THE IMPACT OF DIVORCE

Divorce is the last and, no doubt, most significant factor in the evolution of the traditional family. Much has been made of divorce statistics in the last few years. But frequently those statistics are misreported. Current marriage rates are compared with current divorce statistics; for example, the number of marriages consummated within a given year is compared with the number of marriages dissolved within that same year. A more accurate method would be to track each of the marriages consummated and determine how many are dissolved by divorce. When that is done, we find that the increased divorce rate is caused by baby boomers more than divorces among their parents.

Historically, that fact has already been demonstrated. When baby boomers came of age, divorce statistics went through the roof. The number of divorces rose from 400,000 in 1962 to 1.2 million in 1981.[31] As Landon Jones notes, the increase in the divorce rate occurred not in older couples but in the baby boom generation.

> These were not tired suburban couples finally filing for divorce after sending all their children off. These were young couples divorcing before they even had a chance to get a seven-year itch. The divorce rate has quadrupled for couples under 30 since 1960 and increased 50 percent for couples under 25 in just seven years. One demographer, Tobert Michael of Stanford, has calculated that while men and women in their twenties comprised only about 20 percent of the population, they contributed 60 percent of the growth in the divorce rate in the sixties and early seventies.[32]

Social commentators often blame the liberalization of divorce laws as the primary reason for the increase in the divorce rate. But that change was less a cause of the increase than it was the result of it. Social pressures and opportunities for the baby boom generation were the forces driving the divorce rate up.

DO HALF OF ALL U.S. MARRIAGES END IN DIVORCE?

Social commentators are notorious for stating that half of all U.S. marriages will end in divorce. But is the marriage failure rate really 50 percent?

That percentage comes from comparing two fairly reliable social statistics: the number of marriages licenses issued and the number of divorce decrees issued. The problem arises from comparing the two numbers for any given year.

In 1988, for example, there were 2,389,000 marriages and 1,183,000 divorces. Comparing those two numbers produces the frequently cited 50 percent figure. But only a very small percentage of the people divorced in 1988 were also married in 1988. Comparing 1988 divorces to 1988 marriages is a case of statistically mixing apples and oranges.

Eric Miller in *Future Vision* suggests a better way to estimate the divorce rate. Take the percent of the total adult population who are currently or ever have been married (72 percent) and compare that to the number of people who are currently divorced (9 percent). That produces a 13 percent current divorce rate.

In *100 Predictions for the Baby Boom*, Cheryl Russell predicts that one out of every two baby boom marriages will end in divorce. If that occurs, then that would be a true 50 percent divorce rate.

One reason was an increased number of women in the work force. The rise in divorce closely parallels the increase in the number of women working. Opportunities in employment armed women with economic power, while at the same time diminishing the incentive to stay in marriages and work out their differences. A National Longitudinal Survey of mature women done at Ohio State University found that the higher a woman's income in relation to the total income of her family, the more likely she was to seek a divorce.[33]

Another reason for the increased divorce rate was expectations. Unlike their parents, baby boomers were less committed and less content with compromises.

Previous generations were taught that life is hard, sacrifice is necessary, and unhappiness a cross that sometimes must be borne. But the baby boomers were not willing to make the risky and often painful compromises their parents did. Just as they had great expectations for themselves, they had great expectations for their marriages.[34]

Based on current trends of marriage and divorce, demographer Cheryl Russell predicted that half of all baby boomers will divorce once. She also predicted that one in five will divorce twice.[35] It is little wonder, then, that the number of single-parent households and blended families is on the increase.

Every year, parents of more than one million children divorce, thus effectively cutting one generation off from another. More than half (59 percent) of the baby boom's children will spend at least a year living with only one parent before reaching the age of eighteen.[36] That will certainly affect generational continuity.

But divorce is not the only wall between baby boomers and their children. This generation has seen a sharp increase in the number of children born to unwed mothers. One in five American children is born in what used to be called "illegitimate" situations.[37] The two factors of divorce and illegitimacy have led to a dramatic increase in the number of single-parent households. As in many of the other statistics listed, those social factors hit black and other minority families the hardest.[38]

Divorce and remarriage add an additional twist to the families of the 1990s. Talk shows regularly have discussions about the needs of step-families and blended families as they begin to proliferate. Thirty-five percent of the baby boom's children will live with a stepparent during some part of their childhood.[39]

Forty percent of remarriages of baby boomers include a child from a previous marriage.[40] Unfortunately, the presence of those children adds stress to the remarriages. According to researchers Arland Thornton and Deborah Freedman, remarriages that involve stepchildren are more likely to end in divorce than those that don't.[41] Fully 17 percent of marriages that are remarriages for both the husband and wife and that involve stepchildren break up within three years.[42]

Cheryl Russell concludes in *100 Predictions for the Baby Boom* that

> No one knows what effect divorce and remarriage will have on the children of the baby boom. A few decades ago, children of divorced parents were an oddity. Today they are the majority. The fact that divorce is the norm may make it easier for children to accept their parents' divorce. But what will it do to their marriages in the decades ahead? No one will know until it's too late to do anything about it.[43]

Parents and children in this burgeoning group of stepfamilies find themselves navigating uncharted territory. Contemporary mapmakers of the social scene have called them "neo-nuclear" families—married couples with one or more children in which the multiplicities of parent/child relationships are not strictly biological.[44]

In short, the complexity of family arrangements in the 1990s far exceeds the limited diversity of the family of the 1950s. As baby boomers mature and deal with this diversity and with the dysfunction in their lives, they will (as we will discuss in a later chapter) confront a crisis of relationships. Already as they enter midlife, they are facing a crisis of expectations and struggle with disillusionment.

NOTES

1. Frank Levy and Richard Michel, "Are Baby Boomers Selfish?" *American Demographics*, April 1985, 39–40.
2. Ibid.
3. Ibid.
4. Karen S. Peterson, "$150,000 to Raise a Kid," *USA Today*, 17 January 1990, 1A.
5. Levy and Michel, "Are Baby Boomers Selfish?" 39–40.
6. Landon Jones, *Great Expectations: America and the Baby Boom* (New York: Ballantine, 1980), 335.
7. George Barna, *Frog in the Kettle: What Christians Need to Know About Life in the Year 2000* (Ventura, Calif.: Regal, 1990), 66.
8. Suzy Kalter, *Instant Parents: A Guide for Stepparents, Part-Time Parents and Grandparents* (New York: A & W, 1979), 10.

9. Fitzhugh Dodson, *How to Single Parent* (New York: Harper & Row, 1987), 193.
10. Jones, *Great Expectations*, 192.
11. Ibid., 7.
12. Ibid., 192–93.
13. U.S. Census Bureau.
14. Jones, *Great Expectations*, 197.
15. Betty Friedan, *The Feminine Mystique* (New York: Dell, 1963).
16. Jones, *Great Expectations*, 197.
17. Ibid.
18. Ibid., 3.
19. "Living in the USA," *Public Pulse,* April 1989, 7.
20. Ben Wattenberg, *The Birth Dearth* (New York: Pharos, 1987).
21. U.S. Census Bureau.
22. By the late 1980s, a baby boomlet was felt as the number of births each year began to approach the numbers during the baby boom. However, the boomlet was due not to higher fertility but instead to the millions of baby boom women having children. Although the number of births was up, the fertility rate was still down.
23. Jones, *Great Expectations*, 228.
24. Ibid., 230.
25. Daniel Yankelovich, "The New Breed," *American Family Report,* 1976-77.
26. Neil Postman, *The Disappearance of Childhood* (New York: Dell, 1982), 138.
27. George Masnick and Mary Jo Bane, *The Nation's Families 1960–1990,* cited in Postman, *Disappearance of Childhood,* 121.
28. "Two Million Couples Living Together," *Dallas Times Herald,* October 20, 1977.
29. Jerrold Footlick, "What Happened to the Family" *Newsweek,* special edition, Winter/Spring 1990, 15.
30. Anne Remley, "From Obedience to Independence," *Psychology Today,* October 1988, 56–59.
31. National Center for Health Statistics, "Advance Report of Final Divorce Statistics, 1983," *NCHS Monthly Vital Statistics Report* 34, no. 9, 26 December 1985, Table 1.
32. Jones, *Great Expectations*, 215.
33. Ibid., 216.
34. Ibid., 219.
35. Cheryl Russell, *100 Predictions for the Baby Boom* (New York: Plenum, 1987), 18.
36. Statistic from demographer Arthur J. Norton, cited in "Children in Flux," Opener, *American Demographics,* September 1983, 14. Also, the Congressional Research Service estimated in the mid-1980s that a child born then stood a 60 percent chance of being reared through at least one separation, and a 20 percent chance of going through two. John Koten, "The Shattered Middle Class: A Once Tightly Knit Middle Class Finds Itself Divided and Uncertain," *Wall Street Journal* (9 March 1987), 23.
37. National Center for Health Statistics, "Advance Report of Final Natality Statistics, 1984," *NCHS Monthly Vital Statistics Report* 35, no. 4 (18 July 1986).
38. Jones, *Great Expectations*, 220.
39. Arthur J. Norton, "Children in Flux," 14.

40. Arland Thornton and Deborah Freedman, "The Changing American Family," *Population Bulletin* 38, no. 4 (Washington, D.C.: Population Reference Bureau, 1983), 10.

41. Ibid.

42. Lynn K. White and Alan Booth, "The Quality and Stability of Remarriages: The Role of Stepchildren," *American Sociological Review* 50, no. 5, October 1985, 689–98.

43. Russell, *100 Predictions*, 107.

44. "Families: Neo-Nukes," *Research Alert*, 17 August 1990, 6.

SECTION TWO

SEVEN COMING CRISES

CHAPTER FOUR
THE CRISIS OF PURPOSE

Mike turned forty this year. The surprise party didn't seem traumatic, at least at first. Of course there were the obligatory black balloons and black birthday cards. Some brought gag presents such as Geritol and Grecian Formula. Someone even brought him a cane.

But sometime during the birthday party, the joke turned serious. It began to dawn on Mike that here he was, forty years old, and he still hadn't made his mark on the world. All his life, he had been told that he had great potential. But by age forty, just having potential isn't enough. You have to produce.

By the world's standards, he was successful. He had a secure middle management position in a manufacturing corporation. But many of his goals and aspirations were unrealized, and it was becoming clear that most of his dreams would never be fulfilled. He could no longer reassure himself that he was still young and had plenty of time. Suddenly, time seemed to be running out.

Mike had to acknowledge that the gag gifts weren't too far off the mark. He really did need hair coloring. His hair was graying, and there was much less of it than there was just five years ago. A glance in the hallway mirror reminded him that he was no longer the trim athlete in his wedding pictures. The man in the mirror was middle-aged.

By the time the last guest left, Mike's mood had changed from frivolity to despondency. The joke about a midlife crisis at forty wasn't so funny anymore. His mind flooded with questions. Will I ever reach my goals? Were the dreams of my youth unrealistic? Is this all I am ever going to achieve? They haunted Mike as he turned forty, along with millions of other baby boomers.

A TIME OF QUESTIONING

Since 1986, the boom generation has been speeding past the 4-0 barrier at the rate of more than three million a year. Traditionally seen as the time of transition from youth to middle age, the fortieth birthday has prompted boomers toward introspection and self-evaluation.

The leading-edge baby boomers have been the first group to hit this time of transition. Born in the late forties and early fifties, they lived in new houses that were built on new streets, in new neighborhoods, in the new American community known as the suburbs.

When they headed off to school, they sat in new desks and were taught about Dick and Jane by teachers fresh out of college. They grew up with television and lived in a world brimming with promise. In the sixties they graduated from high school and enrolled in college in record numbers. Then they landed jobs with good salaries in a still-expanding economy and bought homes before housing prices and interest rates went through the roof.

Unlike the baby boomers who were born after them, the leading edge achieved, in large part, the American dream. It wasn't that they were smarter or more talented; they were just born earlier.

But even though they have achieved a degree of financial success, many middle-aged boomers are beginning to encounter a crisis of purpose. They are like the cartoon that appeared in *The New Yorker*. The husband turns to his wife over the breakfast table and says, "The egg timer is pinging. The toaster is popping. The coffeepot is perking. Is this it, Alice? Is this the great American dream?"[1]

Millions in this generation will no doubt repeat those questions in the next two decades. Is this it? Is this the great American dream? And they will ask others: Where is my life going? Is this

Middle-Aging of America

Percent Increase in 35–56 Age Group

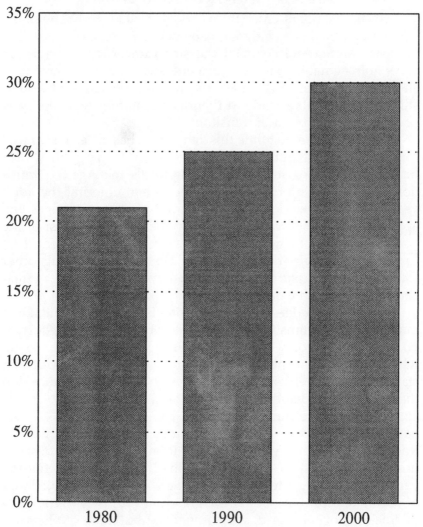

Source: U.S. Census Bureau.

all I am ever going to achieve? In some ways, those are strange questions coming from the leading-edge boomers who enjoy the fruits of the American economy. They have achieved a measure of success, yet they are asking questions that signal a coming crisis of purpose. So why a crisis of purpose? And why now?

FRANTIC AT FORTY-SOMETHING

As its members enter the years of midlife, the baby boom generation remains an enigma. Baby boomers rejected the values of their parents and changed the structure of their families in ways unimaginable to a previous generation. But they must now shoulder adult responsibilities and assume positions of leadership (if they aren't already in them). Put another way, the baby boom stands at a point of transition.

This is not the first time this generation has collectively faced this challenge. When the leading edge began turning thirty, they hit what psychologist Daniel Levinson calls the Age 30 Transition.[2] The struggle of leaving childhood and entering the adult years was being worked out in a period of stagnant wages and appreciating house prices. Ultimately the collective angst of the boom generation turned Gail Sheehy's book *Passages: Predictable Crises of Adult Life* into a runaway best-seller.[3] Among other things, the book assured readers that they were not alone in their confrontation with a major life stage.

The leading edge of this generation is now in the midst of a more significant transition: the midlife transition. Turning forty is no more a predictor of change than turning thirty was. But somewhere in that time period, midlife reevaluation begins. It is a stage in which men and women begin to evaluate and question their priorities and address their dreams and aspirations.

Although the transition is both somber and serious, some have attempted to inject some levity into the discussion. Lawyer Ron Katz found the "yuppie" designation an inaccurate description of his friends' lifestyle, so he coined, somewhat facetiously, yet another acronym to describe boomers at this stage. "No longer rolling stones, but not yet the grateful dead, they're MOSS— middle-age, overstressed, semi-affluent, suburbanites,"[4] he said. According to Katz, "moss" (or mossy, if you prefer the adjective) is what yuppies have become in the 1990s.

Although some social commentators want to discount the existence of a midlife crisis, psychologists and sociologists assure us it does exist. It isn't merely media hype or self-fulfilling prophecy. During the years of midlife, a substantial reevaluation is taking place.

BABY BOOMERS TURN TO MOSS

According to Ron Katz, the average MOSS is:

- 41 years old; more overstressed than overworked; affluent but doesn't feel that way.

- has been married twice to virtually the same person; has 2.5 children (two biological, .5 step); hires three child care persons a year.

- takes most vacations with at least two family members to places previously visited; owns at least one publication about cholesterol; understands why not everyone gets to the top; sees the benefits skin moisturizer bestows on society.

- is beginning to understand why the world hasn't changed more over the past 25 years; hopes that the world changes somewhat less over the next 30 years.

- is principally focused on children, many named Jennifer and Jason.

Source: "Aging of a YUPPIE, the Making of MOSS," *Dallas Times Herald*, 15 June 1989, E-1.

THE MIDLIFE TRANSITION

In actuality, the transition to midlife is gradual. There are no major landmarks or signposts that signal our entry into that new and uncharted domain. Perhaps that is why there are so many jokes about turning forty even though nothing of any significance actually happens on our fortieth birthday. Turning forty provides a visible demarcation of a gradual process.

The onset of a midlife crisis may be sudden and noticeable or gradual and barely perceptible according to psychiatrist Michael Nichols.

Somewhere around the age of forty men and women suffer a profound personal crisis. For some, the routine of everyday life builds to boredom and despair, for which they anxiously seek reasons and from which they search for escape. For others, life slides by unnoticed until some rash act or unexpected setback —an affair or a promotion that falls through—forces them to recognize that something in dreadfully wrong.[5]

Most people are too focused on external challenges in early adulthood to notice the internal changes taking place within them. They are busy starting careers, starting marriages, and starting families to focus much of their conscious energy on their personal selves. But by the forty-something years, questions of reevaluation begin to surface.

In the beginning, feelings of discontent may be vague and barely discernible—perhaps a nagging feeling that something is amiss. For other people, the source of discontent may surface because of a specific failure or setback, such as a lost job, a missed promotion, or a struggling marriage.[6]

Bob had always planned to become head of the marketing department of the computer software firm where he worked. He was its best salesman, and he assured himself that he had the leadership qualities the company needed in that position. So he was shocked and angry when the company named another salesman (who was five years his junior) to take over the department. Nearly overnight his chances for career advancement had been stymied, and Bob began to ask himself what he had done wrong.

BIOLOGICAL CAUSES

Some have wondered if the cause of a midlife crisis is biological. Could it be that hormonal changes actually stimulate soulsearching and reevaluation? So far, at least, attempts to correlate the emotional changes with hormonal changes have been inconclusive. Both men and women experience glandular changes too late in life to explain a midlife crisis. Generally women "do not encounter the first changes in their menstrual cycle until their mid-forties and do not reach menopause until about age fifty. Men do not undergo a shift in testosterone levels until they reach the late forties and early fifties."[7]

That does not mean that biology is completely unrelated to a midlife transition. The loss of physical prowess is a significant concern, especially for men. And biological factors are even more significant for women. Approaching forty means that the childbearing years are coming to an end (for women, but not necessarily for men). Many women begin to feel an intense "baby hunger"[8]

Developmental Periods in Early and Middle Adulthood

Late Adulthood

LATE ADULT TRANSITION

Culmination of Middle Adulthood
Age 50 Transition
Entering Middle Adulthood

MIDLIFE TRANSITION

Settling Down
Age 30 Transition
Entering the Adult World

EARLY ADULT TRANSITION

Childhood and Adolescence

Source: Daniel Levinson, *The Seasons of a Man's Life*, 57. Used by permission.

and begin to question the choices they made in their early adult years.

Jane graduated from medical school more than a decade ago, and in that time had developed a lucrative practice in pediatrics. She had put off marriage and childbearing to concentrate on building her practice. Suddenly it hit her one day that unless she quickly found a mate and started a family, the only children she would ever care for would be other people's.

PSYCHOLOGICAL CAUSES

Although biological factors may have some bearing on the midlife crisis, the primary reason is psychological. In the early 1970s, social psychologists began to document the existence of regular states of personality development in adulthood. These life stages were documented by Daniel Levinson in *The Seasons of a Man's Life.* That foundational book gave rise to such popular books as Sheehy's *Passages: Predictable Crises of Adult Life* and Merser's *Grown Ups: A Generation in Search of Adulthood.*

In his book, Daniel Levinson described a number of developmental stages in adult life. He delineates an early adult era from mid-twenties to late thirties. He also discusses a middle adult era from mid-forties to early sixties. What is in-between is what he calls the years of midlife transition. He sees those years as a bridge between young adulthood and becoming a senior member of one's occupational world.

In his preface, Daniel Levinson says, "Adults hope that life begins at 40—but the great anxiety is that it ends there."[9] Fears that that is true is one of the reasons baby boomers find themselves "frantic at forty-something." They are making a transition from the years of their youth to a time of adulthood without any hope or optimism.

SEASONS OF A MAN'S LIFE

Levinson's study focused exclusively on men between the ages of thirty-five and forty-five (born between 1923 and 1934) from a variety of occupations.

For the great majority of men—about 80 percent of our subjects—this period evokes tumultuous struggles within the self and with the external world. Their Mid-life Transition is a time of moderate or severe crisis. Every aspect of their lives comes into question, and they are horrified by much that is revealed. This, of course, leaves 20 percent who apparently did not suffer any significant crisis in their personal lives.[10]

QUESTIONING ASSUMPTIONS

In his study, Levinson argued that the 20 percent who did not encounter "tumultuous struggles" were in a state of denial and would go through that transition eventually. That raises the first of two assumptions in these studies.

Although the stages and themes documented by these studies are descriptive, they are by no means normative. I would reject a deterministic model that predicts that everyone will go through a certain stage. In writing an earlier book on the subject of death and dying, I found that not all people go through the same psychological stages of grief. Christians, for example, who have come to terms with their own mortality and the mortality of their loved ones can face death and agree with the apostle Paul that it is better "to be absent from the body and present with the Lord."[11] Likewise, a person who has come to grips with his or her place in the world may not face a wrenching midlife crisis.

A second assumption has to do with the subjects of these studies. The major studies of adult development (including Levinson's study) used male subjects born before the Depression of the 1930s. Comparable studies for women were not done, and studies of baby boomers have not been done. The men studied (born in the 1920s and early 1930s) have at least three things in common. They grew up in stable families; they had realistic goals for their lives; and they became adults in an expanding economy. Few experienced divorces in their families. Most had simple goals such as "being able to provide for their families" and "being a good father." They also built their careers in a flourishing economic climate.

Those assumptions are not true for the baby boom generation. They grew up in less stable families and are rearing families in a world where divorce is common. Baby boomers have much greater expectations and thus have personal goals that are much more difficult to fulfill. A baby boomer dreamed of being a millionaire by the age of thirty, of being the president of a Fortune 500 company, of being the first woman astronaut. As we will see from the research, the fulfillment, or the lack of fulfillment, of those goals affects the way a person deals with the time of midlife transition.

Such differences make it difficult to directly apply the studies to the boom generation. Although some investigators argue that talk about a true midlife "crisis" is overblown,[12] most believe the current generation will be even more susceptible to a crisis than the previous.

MAJOR THEMES IN MIDLIFE

In his research, Levinson discovered a number of themes that surface in this universal rite of passage from the early to middle adult years. Five of those themes are relevant to our discussion here:

1. New roles and responsibilities
2. Dealing with death
3. A culminating event
4. Intense introspection
5. Leaving a legacy

1. *Midlife transition involves adapting to new roles and responsibilities.* By the time you are in your thirties, you are expected to think and behave like a parent. You can postpone that for a while, and the boom generation has been fairly successful at postponing adulthood by extending the period called "youth." They extended adolescence into their twenties and even into their thirties. But now they are facing different and more demanding sets of roles and expectations. They are taking senior positions in their jobs and must provide care for both their children and their aging parents.

A man in his forties is usually regarded by people in their twenties as a full generation removed. He is seen more as a parent than as a brother. In the mind of those who are younger, he is "Dad" rather than "buddy." That message comes first as a surprise and then as an irritation to a man in midlife.[13]

Even before Tom turned forty, he started to feel old. He can remember the day he started feeling that way. It happened when one of the newest recruits to the accounting firm was assigned to him for a major tax audit. All day Randy kept calling him "sir." At first it caught Tom off-guard. Everyone in the firm was cordial and casual and rarely used such formalities. By the end of the day, Tom had had enough. He asked Randy to call him Tom. Randy responded, "Well, OK, if that's what you want. But I will have a hard time calling anyone who is nearly my father's age anything but sir."

Another way to look at the transition is to use the definitions of generations used by Spanish philosopher Josè Ortega y Gasset. He identified five generations:[14]

1. Childhood: age 0-15
2. Youth: age 15-30
3. Initiation: age 30-45
4. Dominance: age 45-60
5. Old age: age 60+

The Initiation generation includes the time of midlife transition and leads to the Dominant generation, where individuals are expected to assume the mantle of leadership, authority, and responsibility. According to Ortega y Gasset, the Initiation and Dominant generations are the two most crucial ones. The relationships between them and successful passing of authority from one to another affect the fate of society. During the 1990s and the early part of the twenty-first century, the transition from the older generation to the younger generation will occur and has already begun.

2. *Midlife transition involves facing one's mortality.* By midlife we become increasingly aware of death. Living in a death-denying culture shields us from a sense of our own mortality. And being young further heightens our sense of indestructibility. Teenagers and young adults tend to think of themselves as bulletproof and destined for immortality.

But by the age of forty, we have seen many people, not much older than ourselves, succumb to cancer and heart attacks. Many have seen death in their own family. The death of a parent is a clear signal that we are now on our own. It also reminds us how short life really is.

People going through this transition not only face a crisis of mortality; they face a crisis of growing old. Baby boomers are entering what I call "the ache age." A vigorous exercise is followed by hurting muscles that seem to stay sore longer. Cuts and bruises that used to heal almost overnight take much longer to heal. Such physiological reminders also focus our attention on our inevitable mortality.

Dr. Elisabeth Kubler-Ross has identified the five different stages of grief.[15] Although they describe the psychological stages of a patient who is dying, they correlate remarkably with the feelings people go through in midlife. The crisis of growing old frequently surfaces stages of denial, anger, bargaining, depression, and acceptance.

3. *Midlife transition surfaces after a culminating event.* It serves as a marker for a conclusion of young adulthood. It may be something obvious, such as a promotion or dismissal from a job. But it also might be something that no one else would be able to identify, not even our spouse. It is a milestone that makes us see that one of our life's dreams is not going to be realized and provides an estimate for future success or fulfillment.

In his book, Daniel Levinson argues that our dreams are so compelling that nothing short of total success will satisfy us. In other words, there is no such thing as modest success. Frequently, the culminating event is seen as evidence of flawed success and often as total failure.

To those on the outside looking in, a man may seem to have reached the pinnacle of success. But they can't see into our irrational mind. We often have dreams that are hopelessly unrealistic, especially in youth. A man may be the president of a very successful company but nevertheless feels like a failure because his dream was to be president of the United States. He may be athletic and successful, but health and wealth may not be enough.

Those things weren't for John. In high school, he was a star basketball player recruited by major colleges. Stardom increased in college. John was selected to the conference All-Star team, and even received a mention in *Sports Illustrated.* But the next step never came. No NBA team drafted him, and suddenly his days of playing basketball were over.

Today John heads a real estate company, runs marathons, and plays in local Hoop-It-Up Tournaments. Anyone who knows John thinks he is a success. But John doesn't feel that way. His goal of being an NBA player was never realized. Now that his company is beginning to flounder in a soft real estate market, he feels like a failure.

4. *Midlife transition involves intense introspection.* A consistent pattern of adult life is an early struggle in adulthood to achieve a measure of success followed by a midlife appraisal of one's values and philosophy of life. A man around forty begins to reassess the meaning of life and begins reconsidering the fate of his youthful dreams. He is asking major questions such as: Is this all I am going to do for the rest of my life? or, Is this all I am going to achieve?

Many people find that what they thought would make them happy isn't. They enjoyed law school and the first few years of practicing law. But the thought of being a lawyer for the rest of their life is not fulfilling. They enjoyed the first few years of selling life insurance, but the thought of doing that for another thirty years sounds more like torture than a career.

This is a time when a man shines a light on his accomplishments and sets an agenda for the second half of life. He may or may not make major mid-course corrections, depending on the evaluation.

5. *Midlife transition involves leaving a legacy.* As a man comes to grips with his own mortality, inevitably he has a desire for immortality, which is "one of the strongest and least malleable of human motives."[16] One form of immortality may be achieved by leaving behind a legacy. One is reminded of Woody Allen's quip that he didn't want to be immortal by leaving something behind;

he wanted to be immortal by not dying. But since that is not possible, an individual seeks to leave a legacy, and that usually forms the core of the second half of a person's life.

Successful resolution of midlife comes from determining what legacy—possessions, memories, ministry—a man will leave behind. It may encompass family, work, or all of society. It may involve contributions as parent, spouse, leader, or mentor. The elements of that legacy define the path a man will take in the second half of his life.

SEASONS OF A WOMAN'S LIFE

Although the studies of midlife reveal the potential struggle of men, they give little insight into the transitions women face. The studies done by Daniel Levinson, for example, focused on men a generation older than the men born during the baby boom. Nevertheless, they are still instructive in what struggles may lie ahead for male baby boomers. On the other hand, making predictions for female baby boomers based upon those studies would be very difficult.

Comparable predictions for women are extremely difficult to make because similar studies for women have not been done. Psychiatrist Michael Nichols said, "My guess is that women have as many problems as men but, because women's lives are more complicated with multiple role demands, their crises are more variable than men's."[17]

Women's experiences will no doubt be similar to those men face, especially since the current generation of women has entered the work force in record numbers and therefore exposed themselves to some of the same stresses and influences of men in the work force.

Women, however, face an additional stress. In the 1990s they are asking questions about their place in society. Should they pursue the Superwoman image of the 1970s and 1980s and continue their careers? Or should they reject that image as an unrealistic feminist ideal and settle down to rear their families? Those are but two of many questions women are asking as they enter midlife.

QUESTIONING PRIORITIES

The conflicts baby boom women face in midlife were well-illustrated in a *Time* cover that appeared just as the 1990s were about to begin. The cover story and subtitle read, "Women Face the '90s: In the '80s they tried to have it all. Now they've just plain had it. Is there a future for feminism?"[18]

The editors opened the article with a series of advertisements aimed at women. Here is a 1977 ad for Boeing: "She had breakfast with the national sales manager, met with the client from 9 to 11, talked to an industry luncheon, raced across town to the plans board meeting and then caught the 8:05 back home."[19] Compare that to a recent ad for *Good Housekeeping:* "My mother was convinced the center of the world was 36 Maplewood Drive. Her idea of a wonderful time was Sunday dinner. She bought UNICEF cards, but what really mattered were the Girl Scouts . . . I'm beginning to think my mother really knew what she was doing."[20]

Do you see the change? We were supposedly exchanging the image of the supermom for that of the superwoman. What happened to the accolades that are supposed to be given to the liberated woman in a tailored suit and floppy bow tie climbing the corporate ladder? Are women in the 1990s becoming so exhausted with "having it all" that they are beginning to look back nostalgically to an era of traditional families and traditional values?

Women of the baby boom face a crisis of purpose in the 1990s as they seek to accept or reject the values they adopted in their youth. Many rejected the value system of their mothers and embraced (at least in part) the goals and ideals of the feminist revolution. Others longed for the traditional family of their youth but were forced by economic realities to stay in the work force while rearing their children.

But during the 1990s, women, like their male counterparts, will be forced to reassess their values. This decade will be a time when the fast track meets the Mommy track, when the time clock meets the biological clock.

When she left her job writing advertising copy to have a baby, Patricia wondered if she would miss the office. She wondered if she would be bored at home rearing children. Her mother had been a homemaker, but times had changed and she wondered if she could be content staying at home.

She even began to envy and resent her husband, Tim. His life was not upset to any great degree when they decided to have a family. He continued to work as an advertising account executive. Of course, he would talk about how he got less sleep and had more chores around the house. But she was the one who bore the brunt of the new demands placed upon the family.

After their son was born, Patricia decided to work part-time writing copy and editing manuscripts. Putting together a home office—complete with computer, modem, fax machine, and copier—added some excitement to Patricia's life. Juggling parenting responsibilities and editorial deadlines was more difficult than she anticipated; however, the chance to work again was worth it, and it provided extra income to pay off many of the debts that grew during her absence from the work force.

Patricia worked hard to hold it all together, but she knew that she couldn't do it if they had another child. One child and a part-time job with demanding editorial deadlines was hard enough. Two children would be impossible.

One day she noticed that her period was late, and she realized she was probably pregnant again. Waves of depression crashed over her soul. Though she was grateful that they would have another child, she knew her life as a part-time editor was over, at least for a while. She would have to devote herself full-time to being a mother and homemaker. She wondered if she could be the full-time mother her mother was. But more to the point, she really didn't want to be the full-time mother her mother had been.

THE MOMMY WARS

An internal conflict over a woman's place in the world is difficult enough, but now journalists are finding evidence of a growing conflict between women. They call it "the Mommy Wars." A *Newsweek* article titled "Mommy vs. Mommy" noted that feuds and conflicts define an era. This one may define the late 1980s and 1990s.

> In the '60s, it was hippies versus rednecks. In the '70s, the decade of the women's movement, it was women against men. By the mid-'80s, and now into the '90s, it's mothers against mothers—more precisely, mothers who stay at home against mothers who work. This conflict is played out against a backdrop of frustration, insecurity, jealousy and guilt. And because the enemies should be allies, the clash is poignant.

The article goes on to tell the story of two women:

Elaine Cohen, an executive with a New York television company, moved to suburban Westchester County when her son was 3 years old. Although she had a full-time babysitter while she worked, she wanted to find a play group for him. It should have been easy, but it wasn't. "I called everywhere," she says. But the mothers she spoke with made it very clear that children with babysitters weren't welcome. "As soon as I said that I was a working mother, it was as if I had a disease."

Seven hundred miles away, near Chicago, Joanne Brundage ran into very different problems. Brundage quit her job as a letter carrier to take care of her two children. After a few busy weeks, a friend telephoned and, busy with the baby, Brundage didn't pick up the phone until the fourth ring. "Oh . . . sorry," drawled her friend. "Did I interrupt a crucial moment in your soap opera?"[21]

Women in the 1990s feel caught between the horns of a social dilemma. Should they be in the work force, or should they be at home? Whether in a career or staying at home to rear kids, women face nagging doubts about their place in the world. And those feelings are accentuated by the latest round of mommy wars in the 1990s.

The stay-at-home mother feels torn. She is delighted that she can be at home rearing a family and is doing so because she believes it is best for her children. She is continuing the family traditions of her grandmother and mother. But unlike her mother, she is probably surrounded by neighbors who do not stay at home. Many other mothers go off to work while she stays home. The UPS man drops everyone's packages at her house. Her phone number is the one schools, doctors, even businesses call in emergencies. And she feels as if the world is passing her by while she tries to keep up with the demands of her husband and children.

The working mother faces a different but no less wrenching set of struggles. Like most of the mothers in her generation, she grew up in a home with a breadwinner husband and homemaker wife. Often she must fight off inevitable feelings of guilt because she is not spending the kind of time with her kids that her mother spent with her. She laments that her children may be growing up without her. She missed her child's first step and her child's first word. Either out of economic or psychological necessity, she feels that her place is in the work force, but she still can't help wondering if she made the wrong choice.

THE ROOTS OF THE MODERN WOMAN'S CRISIS

The conflict that women feel in the 1990s is born of substantial changes in our society. Changes in the area of sociology and ideology have left modern women feeling uncertain about their role in society and unappreciated by members in society.

The sociological change occurred when we moved from being an agricultural society to an industrial society. That change affected men and their work, but it has had an even more profound effect on women and their role.

In an agrarian society, a woman could be successful by marrying well. Sociologist Tony Campolo put it this way:

> It used to be fairly simple to figure out what a woman had to do to be successful. She had to marry a decent, hardworking, successful man. The "better" she married, the more successful she would be. Her teenage years were aimed at developing those traits which would make her a desirable marital partner, because men in the rural society of bygone generations demanded far more than physical attractiveness and a pleasant personality in a potential mate. Not that good looks and a congenial manner were unimportant, but a young, aspiring farmer was also looking for someone who could cook, sew, keep house, milk cows, help in the planting, and perform a host of other chores that were part of a well-run farm. A young man was told that beauty was only skin deep; if he was awed by the physical attractiveness of some woman, those who cared about his future would ask, "Can she bake a cherry pie, Billy Boy, Billy Boy?"[22]

When America became an industrial society, many of the previously important requirements were left behind, especially as modern technology reduced some of the toil at home. It was no longer necessary for a homemaker to spend all day in the kitchen cooking, since food was processed and packaged. It was no longer necessary to spend all day washing dishes and clothes. There were dishwashers and washing machines to reduce the amount of time these functions used to require.

That does not mean today's homemaker isn't busy. Just the opposite. She must perform roles ranging from cook to maid to chauffeur to tutor to hostess. And she must do all of that without the help of neighbors or an extended family.

She can no longer gain a sense of personal worth by performing those essential tasks which belonged to her in the agrarian society. Increasingly, her self-image has become dependent on her husband's opinion of her. Now, more than ever, he is the significant other who provides her with whatever sense of success she possesses. If he thinks she is a wonderful person, then she will view herself that way. But if he regards her as an unattractive, uninteresting, and worthless person, in all probability, she will end up feeling like a failure."[23]

That is the curious irony of today's modern woman. In one sense, she enjoys the benefits of modern technology that reduce the toil of keeping a house and family. But it is also that technology that reduces her self-esteem as a homemaker.

The second change has been in the area of ideology. Not only has there been a major social change here; there has also been a major philosophical and ideological change that has affected women. In 1963, Betty Friedan launched the modern feminist movement with *The Feminine Mystique.* As we noted in chapter 3, the early success of the feminist movement was due in large part to the fact that Friedan's comments resonated with women (especially baby boom women) and therefore attracted a following.

Friedan argued that technological advances had diminished the challenge and time involved in caring for a home, and that there was little fulfillment to be found in living vicariously through one's husband or children. She argued that American women were the victims of the "feminine mystique," which perpetuated a false stereotype that women could "find fulfillment only in sexual passivity, male domination, and nurturing maternal love."[24]

Her critique rang true for many women who believed that they did indeed have to live their lives by staying in the background and serving their husbands and children. They thought there should be more to life than living in the shadow of someone else.

The baby boom generation, growing up in the 1950s, came to believe that they were special. So it is not surprising that baby boom women accepted Friedan's central thesis and sought more in life than becoming "just a homemaker." Many entered the work force out of economic necessity but also adopted at least part of the feminist ideology.

The result is that women who would never identify them-selves as feminists still feel the tension described by Betty Frie-dan. Women in the work force and women at home feel the force of the argument and struggle with their role in society.

The consequence is that women in our society spend a fair amount of their conscious time wondering where their place should be. Women in the work force wonder if they should be at home, and women at home wonder if they should be in the work force.

The conflict is difficult enough for a secularly-minded per-son, but I have found that it can become even more intense for a Christian woman. The reason is simple: more is at stake. She is not just asking if what she is doing will make her happy. Most Christian women are also asking, Is this what the Lord is calling me to do? They struggle not only with their own happiness but with God's direction in their life.

Regardless of their religious background, though, women are facing a crisis of purpose in the 1990s. The time of midlife transition is enough to surface questions, but women must work out their answers to these difficult questions against the back-drop of substantial sociological and ideological changes in our society.

A FUTURE CRISIS OF PURPOSE

Both men and women will face a crisis of purpose in the next two decades as they enter into the years of midlife transition. Ideally, a successful transition has both an inward and an out-ward component. Men and women must first focus inward as they analyze their goals and aspirations. But once they have re-directed their lives, they can focus outward on others: friends, family, and society. They can rear their children and prepare them for the future. They can provide care and comfort to their aging parents. They can leave a legacy of service and philanthro-py behind to make society a better place.

A key issue is whether the boom generation will coalesce into a definable group and experience midlife collectively or indi-vidually. Ken Dychtwald, author of *Age Wave*, doesn't believe that the baby boom will go through a typical midlife crisis. In-stead, he argues, this generation will set the tone for society by redefining the notion of aging and giving middle age an aura of youth.[25]

Ross Goldstein agrees. In *Fortysomething: Claiming the Power and Passion of Your Midlife*, he notes that boomers have lived through such social upheavals as the civil rights movement, the Vietnam War, and Watergate. He calls boomers "children of change" and predicts that they will have a smoother transition into midlife.[26] Echoing that idea is Cheryl Merser, author of *Grown Ups: A Generation in Search of Adulthood*. She believes boomers have already had a difficult "passage" into adulthood, so they should have an easier transition into midlife.[27]

Though such an optimistic view is possible, it seems more likely that baby boomers will encounter midlife as individuals rather than collectively as a generation. Psychiatrist Michael Nichols wrote *Turning Forty in the '80s* because he found boomers struggling with the transition. As a director of outpatient psychiatry, he was concerned about the number of thirty-five-to-forty-five year-olds coming in for treatment. Nichols says, "What interested me was that they were as profoundly troubled as my other patients, but there was nothing really wrong with them, except they were struggling with the transition from youth to middle age. I believe the baby boomers are having a harder time with that transition."[28]

His explanation for their difficulty parallels issues already discussed. The boom generation expected upward mobility and peak earnings in their forties. Instead, they face plateaued careers and stagnant wages. How they fare with this major life transition will depend not only upon how they handle the impending crisis of purpose but how they handle another looming crisis of disillusionment.

NOTES

1. Cartoon reprinted in article by Daniel B. Moskowitz, "The Trappings of Success—Or Just a Trap?" *Business Week*, 6 February 1989.
2. Daniel J. Levinson et al., *The Seasons of a Man's Life* (New York: Knopf, 1978).
3. Gail Sheehy, *Passages: Predictable Crises of Adult Life* (New York: Bantam, 1974).
4. "Aging of a Yuppie, The Making of MOSS," *Dallas Times Herald*, 15 June 1989, E-1.
5. Michael P. Nichols, *Turning Forty in the Eighties: Personal Crisis, Time for Change* (New York: Simon & Schuster, 1986), 17.
6. Ibid., 19.
7. Ibid., 26.

8. Ibid., 20.
9. Levinson, *The Seasons of a Man's Life*, ix.
10. Ibid., 199.
11. 1 Corinthians 5:3.
12. Lois M. Tamar, "Modern Myths About Men at Midlife: An Assessment," in *Midlife Myths: Issues, Findings and Practice Implications*, ed. Ski Hunter and Martin Sundel (Newbury Park, Calif.: Sage, 1989).
13. Levinson, *Seasons*, 28.
14. Quoted in *The Seasons of a Man's Life*.
15. Elisabeth Kubler-Ross, *On Death and Dying* (New York: Macmillan, 1969).
16. Levinson, *The Seasons of a Mans's Life*, 215.
17. Nichols, *Turning Forty in the Eighties*, 27.
18. "Women Face the 90s," *Time*, 4 December 1989.
19. Claudia Wallis, "Onward, Women!" *Time*, 4 December 1989, 80.
20. Ibid.
21. Nina Darnton, "Mommy vs. Mommy," *Newsweek*, 4 June 1990, 64.
22. Anthony Campolo, *The Success Fantasy* (Wheaton, Ill.: Victor, 1980), 90.
23. Ibid.
24. Betty Friedan, *The Feminine Mystique* (New York: Dell, 1963), 37.
25. Ken Dychtwald, *Age Wave* (New York: Bantam, 1990).
26. Quoted in Bob Porter, "Baby Boomers May Face Midlife Without a Crisis," *Dallas Times Herald*, 14 May 1991, D-1.
27. Cheryl Merser, *Grown Ups: A Generation in Search of Adulthood* (New York: New American Library, 1987).
28. Ann Zimmerman, "Fortysomething and Frantic," *Dallas Times Herald*, 15 June 1989, E-4.

CHAPTER FIVE
THE CRISIS OF DISILLUSIONMENT

Dan felt like a failure. He was energetic, creative, and resourceful. But he just couldn't pull it off. He couldn't bring in enough income. Therefore, his wife, Susan, had to go back to work. He wondered what was wrong. After all, when he was growing up, his dad went off to work and his mom stayed home. They lived in a nice house, drove two cars, went on annual vacations, and always seemed to have enough money.

Dan's dad was not unique. Every dad on the block went to work while their wives stayed home to rear the children. And, more to the point, everyone on the block was a typical middle-class family.

Times surely had changed. Dan had one full-time job at a department store and worked the swing shift at a convenience store. He still could not make ends meet, and Susan took a job at a nearby greeting card shop. Yet even with three paychecks, Dan and Susan were struggling financially. They were up to their necks in debt and probably would never be able to afford to buy a house.

Dan and Susan are but two of millions of baby boomers who are facing a growing crisis of disillusionment. Having grown up in a world that fed and nurtured their level of expectations, they are facing a world much different from the one in which they were raised. This crisis of disillusionment could also be called a crisis of "broken promises" since they came to expect that in adulthood they would be privileged to enjoy the fruits of the American dream. Instead, they are tasting the bitter fruit of despair and disillusionment.

As noted in the introductory chapters, the seeds of these circumstances were sown in earlier decades. During the 1980s they took root and grew, creating a different set of circumstances for this generation in the 1990s.

A GENERATION DIVIDED

Although this situation has affected all baby boomers, it has hit one segment especially hard: the trailing edge. The members of this generation who were born during the boom's later years (1955-1964) have not fared as well as their older brothers and sisters.

Psychologist Kevin Leman has written about the effects of birth order in a single family.[1] The oldest child tends to be serious, responsible, even driven. The youngest child tends to be more carefree—sometimes becoming the family comic. The order of birth in a single family can often be a great predictor of personality traits.

In *Baby Boomers*, Paul Light observes that "generations may be subject to the same kinds of birth-order effects that social psychologists find in families."[2] Just as the firstborn in a family receives a disproportionate amount of parental attention and nurturance, so firstborn boomers received a disproportionate amount of societal attention and privilege.

In the American "first come-first served" economy, the leading edge found better jobs, better opportunities for career advancement, and better housing prices. The trailing edge found just the opposite.

For example, take housing costs. A couple who bought a house before inflation and interest rates increased would be better off financially than a couple who bought a house at an inflated price. The leading edge bought homes before the prices went through the roof. They invested in an appreciating asset. By

Comparison Between Leading-Edge and Trailing-Edge Boomers

LEADING EDGE BABY BOOMER HOUSEHOLDS (Age 35–44)		
	Households (millions)	Median Income
Total Households	19.323	$34,929
Family Households	15.852	36,836
Non-family Households	3.471	24,586

TRAILING EDGE BABY BOOMER HOUSEHOLDS (Age 25–34)		
	Households (millions)	Median Income
Total Households	20.583	$26,923
Family Households	15.008	28,813
Non-family Households	5.575	22,694

Source: U.S. Census Bureau, 1988.

contrast, the trailing edge bought (or tried to buy) houses that were already inflated. Often coming up with the down payment was difficult, if not impossible.

In general, the earlier someone was born, the better his or her chances of succeeding in the economy. Anyone who doubts that trend need only watch the devastating impact such economic forces are having on the generation following the baby boom. Many "baby busters" cannot find a job that pays them enough to move out of their parents' home. Buying a home of their own seems an impossible dream.

The economic impact on careers is also apparent. The median family income of leading-edge households in 1988 was $34,929. For trailing-edge households it was $26,923.[3] Part of that $8,000 difference is due to career advancement and seniority (people generally tend to earn more as they grow older). But most of the difference is due to timing: the trailing edge arrived at jobs later than the leading edge. Just as being the last to the dinner table can limit your selection of food, so being the last to the job market limited younger boomers' selection of jobs.

NOT EXACTLY THE WONDER YEARS

The seeds of disillusionment for the trailing-edge boomers were sown in the 1960s and 1970s. Unlike their older brothers and sisters, they were not reared in the optimism of the Eisenhower and Kennedy years. Camelot was a historical footnote for them. During their "wonder years," they experienced the assassinations of John Kennedy, Martin Luther King, Jr., and Robert Kennedy. They grew up during the Vietnam War. They saw antiwar protests on nightly television. Leading-edge boomers saw their idyllic visions unravel in the late sixties, but they retained their childhood memories of a world of affluence and optimism. By contrast, trailing-edge boomers growing up in the 1960s saw a different world—a world of shattered dreams and discordant images.

Whereas older boomers grew up in relatively stable families, younger boomers saw the divorce rate climb to unprecedented levels. Television shows about traditional families such as the Andersons and the Cleavers were replaced by sitcoms about single parents such as "Julia" and blended families such as "The Brady Bunch."

By the time younger boomers hit the job market, wages had stagnated. National attention on a potential energy crisis, an Arab oil embargo, and governmental attempts to control inflation made a bad economy worse. Prime entry-level jobs were hard to find, and chances for career advancement seemed slim. Inflation peaked at 18 percent in 1979, and unemployment reached 11 percent in 1982—the highest level since before World War II. Those certainly were *not* the "wonder years."

Yet through the 1980s, boomer optimism buoyed the hope that perhaps tomorrow would be better, as it had been for their parents. Mom and Dad had struggled through the Great Depression and survived World War II to build a better life. Boomers hoped that the same would be true for them too. But, for many, better never came, and they are facing an impending crisis of disillusionment in the 1990s.

Comparing Yuffies
and Yuppies Vocations

How their vocations compare	
YUPPIE	YUFFIE
Brain surgeon	Butcher in a health food store
Corporate lawyer	Junior high civics teacher
Architect	Free-lance house painter
Civil engineer	Bicycle repairman
Interior designer	History museum curator
Starlet	Summer playhouse box office manager

Source: "Yuffies: A Study in Failure," *Dallas Times Herald*, February 26, 1989, F–1.

YUFFIES VERSUS YUPPIES

Always looking for new acronyms to describe a portion of the population, social commentators dubbed these boomers "yuffies"—young, urban failures. Just as the name *yuppie* lacked demographic precision, so also the term *yuffie* is imprecise. Nevertheless, the term reinforces a point made earlier in this book. Not all baby boomers are yuppies. Just the opposite. Most baby boomers are coming face-to-face with disillusionment and downward mobility.

Definitions used in 1985 to describe yuppies and yuffies illustrate the point.[4] Yuppies were defined as twenty-five to thirty-nine-year-olds who live in metropolitan areas, work in professional or managerial occupations, and earn at least $30,000 if living alone and $40,000 if married or living with someone else. Using that definition, there were only four million yuppies—constituting just 5 percent of all baby boomers.

Yuffies were defined as baby boomers making less than $10,000 a year. Although that definition seemed much too restrictive in terms of income, it still defined a full 40 percent of the baby boom generation. In 1985, yuffies were roughly eight times as numerous as yuppies.[5]

Yuffies, and people who feel like yuffies, feel as if they do not measure up. Many, if not most, were born with the trappings of success. Their parents were successful in providing for and rearing a family. But their life took a turn in the opposite direction. Patricia Friedman, author of *Too Smart to Be Rich*, somewhat humorously remarks that "Yuffiehood is like any psychosomatic illness. You're born with a predisposition—to migraine headaches, to ulcers, to failure. All it takes is just the right environment and you're on your way."[6]

According to Friedman, yuffies and yuppies both have great promise and travel similar paths sometimes until early adulthood.

> That road forks at age 30. The yuppies clamber off on the great search for goat cheese and BMWs. And the yuffies just keep keeping on. Life after 30 is just an extension of the flawed questing of the 20s. It's sort of like being trapped in a time warp in your sophomore year of college and never getting out of it.[7]

Frequently the choices that yuffies make are quite noble: to pursue a career in the arts, to do social work in urban areas, to finish a doctorate in English literature. The difficulty comes in financially providing for themselves and their family (if they have one). Often public service and academic preparation have not translated into economic security. And even those who are able to pay the bills feel as if they have not been able to make the same "mark in the world" that their parents did.

A generation with great expectations has had a difficult time coming to grips with what seems like broken promises. Despair is inevitable. Dr. Carol Nadelson of the American Psychiatric Association noted that in 1966 "there were about 16,800 psychiatrists in America. Now, there are more than twice that number—plus thousands more psychologists and psychiatric social workers. . . . These people were told promises can be fulfilled if they worked hard. But they worked hard, and their promises weren't fulfilled."[8]

HOME BITTERSWEET HOME

The American dream has meant different things to different people, but one of the most universal, deeply-held aspects of the dream has been owning a home. A Roper Organization survey in 1989 reported that nearly nine out of ten adults listed "a home that you own" as part of the life they would like to have.[9] That rated nine percentage points ahead of a happy marriage and fourteen points ahead of a car or children.

Not only is home ownership a big part of the American dream; it is part of the American fantasy. A nationwide survey by Spiegel, Inc., found that one out of ten Americans fantasizes about the "house of their dreams" every single day.[10] The dream house has four bedrooms, three bathrooms, two fireplaces, seven closets, three televisions, four telephones, and is a short stroll from the beach. Other amenities include a media/entertainment center, an exercise facility, a library, a spa/whirlpool, a home office, and an indoor/outdoor pool.

If that characterization of American home fantasies is even close to accurate, no wonder more and more boomers are facing a crisis of shattered dreams. The American economy simply did not deliver.

The dream of owning one's own home is a relatively recent one. In 1946—the year the baby boom began—the majority of Americans were renters. Yet within one generation, more than two-thirds of Americans became homeowners.[11] The boom generation, growing up in the midst of this significant transition, came to see home ownership as a right rather than a privilege.

Part of the dream also included living in the suburbs—a geographical region of the country that also is a relatively recent phenomenon. When the GIs returned to America after World War II, they faced an acute housing shortage. Foreclosures on home mortgages during the Great Depression and limited home construction during World War II put the country in a housing crunch.

To meet the need, developers built more than a million new homes every year for the next twenty years (1945-1965).[12] One of the most famous housing tracts was built in Island Trees, Long Island, by William J. Levitt. That first American suburb, later dubbed Levittown, began the pattern for future housing tracts. In *Crabgrass Frontier*, Kenneth Jackson describes the creative and efficient way Levitt assembled those tracts:

> After bulldozing the land and removing the trees, trucks carefully dropped off building materials at precise 60-foot intervals. Each house was built on a concrete slab (no cellar); the floors were of asphalt and the walls of composition rock-board. . . . Freight cars loaded with lumber went directly into a cutting

yard where one man cut parts for ten houses in one day. The construction process itself was divided into 27 distinct steps—beginning with laying the foundation and ending with a clean sweep of the new home. Crews were trained to do one job—one day the white-paint men, then the red-paint men, then the tile layers. Every possible part, especially the most difficult ones, was preassembled in central shops.[13]

The homes were hardly elegant, but they met a crucial need for starter homes and provided young couples with the dream of owning their own home.

The boom generation, on the other hand, hit a housing crunch in the 1970s that was not as easily resolved. When they headed out into the world upon graduation, they found stagnant wages and increasing house prices. As we have already noted, both phenomena were due to the size of the baby boom generation.

The size of the generation was only one reason for rising home prices. The living patterns of the boomers exacerbated the problem. Three lifestyle patterns are especially relevant. First, baby boomers left the nest earlier than any other generation.[14] Many left for college and never returned home but instead began looking for a home of their own. Second, boomers stayed single longer. Unlike their parents, who married early and then purchased a house, boomers in the 1970s often bought homes as singles, thereby creating an even greater demand on the housing market. Finally, boomers had higher divorce rates, which also created more demand for housing.

Those three patterns converged to increase the demand for housing. From 1960 to 1980, the total number of households grew by at least ten million each decade. To put that dramatic increase in perspective, the rate of increase for households was three times faster than that of the population as a whole.[15]

Other factors that made home ownership more expensive were higher mortgage interest rates, more rigid mortgage qualification standards, and a multitude of land planning and zoning regulations. Many communities created a byzantine structure of restrictive ordinances, time-consuming building permit processes, and land use restrictions, along with other measures that served to limit growth and increase property values.[16] By 1982, President Reagan's Commission on Housing found that "unnecessary regulation of land use and buildings has increased so much over the

Number of Households

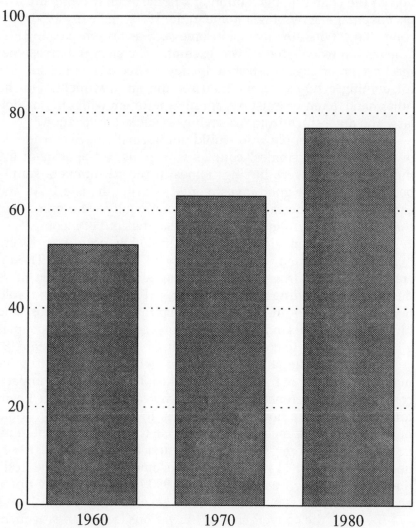

Millions of Households

Source: U.S. Census Bureau.

past two decades that Americans have begun to feel the undesirable consequences: fewer housing choices, limited production, high costs and lower productivity in residential construction." Those regulations, according to the commission, increased the cost of houses sometimes by as much as 25 percent.[17]

A final reason for the increased cost of home ownership involved the changing perception of a home as an investment. The tax advantage of owning a home in the 1970s and early 1980s was compelling. When the federal income tax was first enacted in 1913, "interest on indebtedness" was exempt.[18] Therefore, a homeowner receives a mortgage-interest deduction—effectively a tax subsidy for owning a house rather than renting an apartment. On the other hand, a renter must pay for his apartment with aftertax dollars, and any return from his savings is subject to taxation.[19]

Suddenly, people who would not normally have considered owning a house (singles, couples who preferred apartment living, and so on) were buying homes in record numbers simply because they were good investments.[20] During the late 1970s and early 1980s, net increases in homeowner equity were more than three times larger than total personal savings out of income.[21]

Soon the frenzy become a self-fulfilling prophecy. Rising home prices seemed like a good way to beat inflation. The increased demand drove prices even higher, spurring even more demand.[22] According to one writer, "They bought and sold homes like traders in the pork-belly pit. It was the 1980s, and hundreds of thousands of baby boomers, two-income-couples with ready access to credit, were buying New York real estate."[23]

Taken together, all of those factors worked together to price many couples out of the housing market. To illustrate the impact, compare the difference between buying a new home in Levittown and buying a house in the 1980s. In 1949, a thirty-year-old man purchasing a median-priced house (the median is the midpoint; half the homes sell for more and half sell for less) only needed to commit 14 percent of his income. A new "Cape Cod" house in Levittown went for just $7,990 (with no money down and only $60 dollars a month for mortgage).

By 1983, the convergence of the various factors already mentioned radically altered the equation. Now a thirty-year-old man needed to commit 44 percent of his income to meet the carrying charges on a median-priced house. That same year, 65 percent of all first-time home buyers needed two paychecks to meet their monthly payments.[24]

Fewer Homeowners

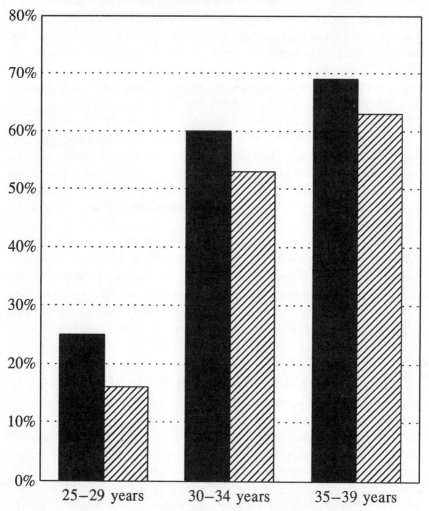

Percent Who Are Homeowners

■ 1973 ☑ 1988

Source: Joint Economic Committee of Congress.

The median home price in 1955 was $13,400. The median price in 1985 rose to $88,900. By the end of the 1980s, the median house price hit $129,800 (and the average home price in 1989 was $159,200).[25] When home prices are this high, large numbers of Americans are priced out of the housing market.

The demographics of first-time home buyers in 1989 further illustrate this point. The median home price for first-time buyers went over the $100,000 mark (actually $105,200) in that year. The average first-time buyer was nearly thirty-something (29.6), and most first-time buyers (87 percent) needed dual incomes to qualify.[26]

The prospects for a typical renter to become a homeowner are discouraging. Apartment rents stabilized during the late 1980s but at record high levels. Only four out of ten young renters had sufficient income to qualify for the mortgage on a median "starter house."[27] Coming up with a down payment was no easier. According to Harvard University's Joint Center for Housing Studies, even with a 10 percent down payment mortgage, only 20 percent of white renters and 4 percent of black renters can afford a typical starter house.[28]

Each year, home ownership rates slip lower and lower. In 1973, one in four people aged twenty-five to twenty-nine years owned a home; by 1988, that rate had fallen to 16 percent. In the thirty- to thirty-four-year-old group home ownership was 60 percent but 53 percent in 1988. And in the thirty-five to thirty-nine age bracket, ownership dropped from 69 percent in 1973 to 63 percent in 1988.[29]

HITTING A CAREER PLATEAU

Not only has home ownership become a broken promise, so has the promise of career advancement. Baby boomers saw their parents' salaries and job opportunities increase, but that has not been the case for them. Wages stagnated in 1973, thus reducing boomer earning potential. By the end of the 1970s, *Fortune* magazine estimated that this generation had effectively lost ten years' income when compared with the earnings of the generation just preceding it.[30]

In the 1970s and 1980s, many couples were able to cope with declining wages by living off two incomes. Many middle-class couples compensated primarily due to the strength of the woman's increased income since men's earnings remained relatively flat during this period. But even the wife's additional income could not forestall the economic impact on families. Young families with two paychecks today earn about the same as a couple that lived on the husband's salary alone in the 1970s.[31]

The problem intensified in the 1990s. The size of the boom generation caused part of the problem (as we have previously noted and will elaborate further in the chapter on financial security). The resulting discrepancy between job supply and job demand first affected the number of entry-level positions that baby boomers could find. Now the mass of boomers find themselves competing for increasingly scarce management-level positions. As one rises in the corporation, the number of management positions decreases as the corporate pyramid narrows. In the early 1980s, economists were writing about the presence of too many people vying for too few management-level positions, causing a bottleneck at the middle management level.[32]

Changes in the corporate world throughout the 1980s exacerbated the problem. Downsizing, streamlining, and merging are just a few of the terms used to describe the twisting of the corporate pyramid into an almost unrecognizable polygon. Driven by the twin goals of improving productivity and enhancing their ability to compete, major corporations have eliminated whole levels of middle and upper management.

This generation often finds itself facing two dismal prospects: career plateauing and the potential of a midlife layoff. Belt-tightening measures in the 1980s forced employees to be content with lower wages and smaller wage increases. One research economist predicts that "salaries will probably barely keep up with the cost of living and taxes. . . . I think we're looking at very modest wage increases in the 1990s."[33] For a generation reared on high expectations, the reality of lower wages and fewer and smaller increases can lead to severe disillusionment.

More troubling for this generation is the very real prospect of a future layoff. As boomers move up the corporate pyramid, many face the grim reality that it is either "up or out." If they are passed over for the next promotion, they may eventually be laid off. A typical dual-income couple could be facing the crisis of a stalled career and a layoff simultaneously, adding untold stress to the family.

Even those who find themselves in a secure and successful career are not exempt from anxiety. They are frequently the most driven and the most insecure. Psychologists have identified the syndrome as the "impostor phenomenon." In 1985, the American Psychological Association even held a symposium on the subject.[34]

The psychologists who identified that phenomenon estimated that as many as 40 percent of young, high achievers suffered from the psychological malady.[35] They were baby boomers (men and women in their twenties and thirties) who were successful in their careers but who felt like failures. They felt vulnerable. A minor mistake or miscalculation in a meeting could send them into depression for days because they always felt vulnerable to exposure and ridicule. Unlike the stereotype of the successful yuppie who confidently believed he deserved his success, the "impostors" feared their next mistake would provide full disclosure of who they were—or were not.

Psychologist Joan Harvey identified a number of species of "impostors."[36] The "workaholics" threw themselves into long hours of work in order to drown their fears of exposure and to compensate for their perceived lack of innate talent and intelligence. The "charmers" used flattery and flirting to achieve their goals rather than hard work and ingenuity. Racing from one crisis to another are the "magical thinkers" who subject themselves to spasms of cramming and fits of anxiety in order to succeed. And "shrinking violets," though longing for praise, manage to deflect recognition from themselves to others.

Ross Goldstein, writer of the column "Dr. Baby Boom," believes that this generation will feel the ambivalent, bittersweet nature of success during the coming years of midlife transition and disillusionment. For the baby boom generation the impostor phenomenon is

> an unresolved struggle to reconcile high achievement with low self-esteem, past values with present lifestyle. Ours isn't the only generation to feel unprepared for power. But it is worse for us. We are the group who would never grow old, the don't-trust-anyone-over-30 set. How do we balance that as we round the age-40 turn? Many will spin out into self-doubt and despair.[37]

The result has been disillusionment not only with careers and salaries but with work itself. In the 1960s and 1970s, pollster Daniel Yankelovich began to document changes in American attitudes toward work. First, he discovered a substantial drop in the number of college students who believe that "hard work always pays off." In the mid-sixties 72 percent of college students subscribed to that view, but by the early seventies, adherents dropped to 40 percent.[38] Yankelovich also found similar patterns among adult Americans. Throughout the following decade, the number of Americans who believed that "hard work always pays off" dropped from a majority to a minority.[39] Americans appear to be growing more disillusioned with their chances of sharing in the blessings and bounty of American life, however hard they work.

THE SHRINKING MIDDLE CLASS

Such economic changes have spawned a significant socio-logical change in American society. If you asked baby boomers, when they were growing up, what economic class their families were in, the nearly universal answer would be the middle class. Even affluent families and families living below the poverty line would probably have a tendency to think of themselves as part of America's middle class.

During the 1950s, nearly six out of ten American families had an income profile that would place them firmly within the middle class.[40] But even families above and below the true middle class contributed to a middle-class values consensus. The percep-tion was that the country was becoming one uniform class with similar tastes and values. An article in *Fortune* in the 1950s said, "The U.S. is becoming a one-class market of prosperous middle-income people" who essentially "buy the same things—the same staples, the same appliances, the same cars, the same furniture, and much the same recreation."[41]

Today most Americans still count themselves as part of the middle class, but that reflects perception more than reality. Econ-omists and demographers may disagree about where to draw the lines for the middle class, but they all agree that the middle class is shrinking and migrating to the income extremes. Harvard Uni-versity's David Bloom says, "The middle class still cuts itself a large slice of the American pie, but the country has moved in the direction of becoming a nation of haves and have-nots, with less in between."[42]

The shrinking of the middle class has initiated the erosion of the middle-class consensus. That consensus has given way to fragmented values and community. Demographers document a pluralization of lifestyles and social attitudes. Advertisers no longer try to reach a mass market because it has been replaced by numerous micro-markets. Parents find fewer mutually agreed-

Rising Cost of Living
Comparison Between 1970 and 1985

	1970	1985
House down payment	$5,320	$20,160
Mortgage payments	17.9% of median family income	29% of median family income
Education at a private, four-year college	29.6% of median family income	40.4% of median family income
Average-priced car	18 weeks of pay	23 weeks of pay

Source: "Middle-Class Squeeze," *U.S. News and World Report,* August 18, 1986.

upon standards and guidelines for rearing their children. Sociologists describe a society losing its sense of community and fragmented in a variety of ways. A *Wall Street Journal* reporter put it this way:

> In short, there is no longer one set of values that broadly fits the bulk of the middle class; there are fewer things that everybody wants. And there are fewer things that everybody feels compelled to do. The notions of self-sacrifice and loyalty that George Bernard Shaw alluded to in his definition of "middle-class morality"—"I have to live for others and not for myself"—have largely given way to middle-class independence. People are more likely to face what Tom Wolfe calls the "problem of overchoice."[43]

A generation used to being part of the vast middle class finds itself walking up a descending economic escalator. Downward mobility coupled with a shrinking middle class is not only affecting society and its values; it creates a psychological gap between expectations and reality.

> Unlike earlier decades of expansion—when all it took to be upwardly mobile was to be lifted by the generally rising economic tide—members of today's middle class find they must work

more to wind up with less. A generation raised with great material expectations has discovered there's a gap between its reach for more satisfaction and what is within its grasp.[44]

BOOMER BLUES

The social and economic changes that have already occurred and will continue to develop throughout the 1990s have set this generation up for the crushing realization of broken promises. A generation expecting the best will have to settle for much less.

For a young generation of high rollers, the stock market crash of 1987 may have been the first taste of bitter downturn. As we enter the *fin de siecle* decade, the middle class will feel the squeeze too. As the lid comes down, relationships, financial goals and career aspirations will all be affected:

• Not everyone who expected to own a home or reach other financial aims will realize these goals.

• Not everyone who expected to attend undergraduate, graduate or professional school will be able to afford it.

• Not everyone who expected to reach career objectives set in earlier, less competitive times, will succeed.

• Not everyone who expected to marry will find a mate.

• Not everyone who expected to be a parent but deferred childbearing will be able to have a family.

• Not everyone who simply expected companionship will find someone to be with.[45]

As those harsh realities come crashing down on baby boomers, they will surface certain predictable emotions and responses. Two likely emotions are depression and envy. Dr. Gerald Klerman of Cornell Medical College found that baby boomers (in this study, those born between 1947 and 1967) were four to five times more likely to be depressed than those born earlier or later.[46] A generation taught to expect great things from life had little emotional cushion when society could not deliver on its tacit promises. Moreover, wrenching emotional experiences are taking place in family systems that provide much less social support.[47] Urbanization, dual family incomes, and the breakdown of the family unit (divorce, separation, and so on) provide less support and encouragement to family members who are discouraged and depressed. Put another way, the psychology of the baby boom generation made it more vulnerable to depression, whereas the sociology of baby boomers made them less able to cope with that depression.

Although all members of the baby boom generation feel the crushing weight of disillusionment, women feel it even more. Surveys of women who were born between 1945 and 1955 show that they struggle even more than men do with depression. According to one writer, "It seems these women have lost the optimism of youth without having gained the equilibrium of age."[48] Reasons for higher rates of depression in women are many. They must come to terms with more issues in their lives than men, and they are affected by hormonal changes more than men. But another reason, relevant to this discussion, is that baby boomer women grew up in a world where they were told they could "have it all."

The feminist movement promised them a prominent place in society, and commercials aimed at upscale women told them that they could be corporate executives and supermoms. Reality didn't turn out to be quite as rosy, according to Dr. Klerman.

> Despite the strides made by the woman's movement, life hasn't been as easy as anticipated for female baby boomers. They grew up in a time of prosperity. Many of them are less well-off than their parents, even though they are working as hard. There's a big gap between expectations and experience. Furthermore, women still earn less than men and juggle housework and child care.[49]

Even those who would consider themselves feminists (only about 33 percent of American women) are expressing their disillusionment with the situation facing them. Writing in a "My Turn" column in *Newsweek*, Kay Ebeling called feminism "the Great Experiment That Failed." She believes that women in her generation were both the perpetrators and the casualties of an ideology that sought to free women but instead enslaved them.[50] *Time* reports:

> Sometimes even the women who participated in the feminist revolution, who shaped their lives according to its ideals, shake their heads and wonder. Call them the "Yes, but . . ." generation. Yes, these women in their 30s and 40s are feminists, but things have not worked out as expected. It is hard for them not to feel resentful: toward society for not coming to the aid of

women in their new roles, toward the movement for not anticipating the difficulties.[51]

Baby boomer women in the 1990s find that they do indeed
have more opportunities, but they also have more stress as they
try to pursue those opportunities. These women are finding it
difficult to "have it all," and, when they do, something in their
lives suffers. A nationwide survey of women asked: "Would you
describe yourself as someone who has a marriage, family, and a
successful career?" American women were divided: 43 percent
said yes, 54 percent said no. When asked, "When women try to
have it all, which do you think suffers most?" women responded:
children (42 percent), marriage (28 percent), and career (12
percent).[52]

THE FAILURE OF FEMINISM

Excerpts from an essay
by Kay Ebeling

To me, feminism has backfired against women. In 1973 I left
what could have been a perfectly good marriage, taking with me
a child in diapers, a 10-year-old Plymouth and Volume 1,
Number One of Ms. Magazine. I was convinced I could make it
on my own. In the last 15 years my ex has married or lived with a
succession of women. As he gets older, his women stay in their
20s. Meanwhile, I've stayed unattached. He drives a BMW. I ride
buses.

Today I see feminism as the Great Experiment That Failed, and
women in my generation, its perpetrators, are the casualties.
Many of us, myself included, are saddled with raising children
alone. The resulting poverty makes us experts at cornmeal
recipes and ways to find free recreation on weekends. At the
same time, single men from our generation amass fortunes in
CDs and real-estate ventures so they can breeze off on ski
weekends. Feminism freed men, not women.

The reality of feminism is a lot of frenzied and overworked
women dropping kids off at day-care centers. If the child is sick,
they just send along some children's Tylenol and then rush off to
underpaid jobs that they don't even like.

Source: "The Failure of Feminism," *Newsweek*, 19 November 1990, 9.

Women responding to the survey may have left out one group of people who suffer when women try to have it all—themselves. The stress on women in the 1990s is significant. For example, consider the ulcer rate among women. In 1966, an American woman was one-twentieth as likely to have an ulcer as an American man. By 1986, women trying to hold down a career and hold together a family had fully half as much chance to end up with a perforated stomach.[53]

Diminishing expectations is just one reason for rising depression among boomers. Another reason is a breakdown of community and family. National surveys indicate that the rate of depression has increased nearly tenfold in the last two generations.[54] Psychologist Martin Seligman suggests that the increase is due to cultural changes. Earlier generations faced life's problems with the support of family and community. Today, baby boomers generally must face such problems alone.

Seligman found striking differences between non-Western, developing cultures and our own. Depression in other countries surfaces much less often than it does here and is usually tied to physiological factors. Other cultures have mechanisms, even rituals, that prevent feelings of depression from developing.

But we don't have to look to Third World cultures to see the benefit of community. Seligman cites the research done on the mental health of the Old Order Amish who live in Lancaster County, Pennsylvania. They are a nineteenth-century farming culture (no electricity, no automobiles) with strong religious and family ties. Although their rate of depression due to physiological factors (bipolar depression: manic-depressive disorder) is comparable to that of nearby Baltimore residents, their rate of other types of depression (unipolar depression) is about one-tenth that of people living in Baltimore.[55] That is the same rate found in our society approximately two generations ago.

Seligman believes that the social and cultural changes of the last few decades have made this generation more vulnerable to depression.

We live for the first time in an age of personal control, or as Ronald Reagan dubbed it, "The Age of the Individual." At least four historical forces have converged to make this happen. The first two—the rise of "personalized" mass production, and general prosperity—have exalted the self; the other two—the assassinations of public leaders and the loss of faith in God and family—have weakened our commitment to larger social institutions. And one untoward consequence of this convergence has been a huge increase in depression.[56]

Personalized mass production increased the number of consumer choices (creating another crisis, which we will address in the next chapter) while rising affluence increased individual options. Soon the self was elevated above the community, and this country became a nation of individual selves. Always individualistic, Americans raised the cult of the individual to even higher levels, breaking attachments to family, church, and society. That newfound freedom has extracted a price though: higher rates of depression when expectations do not match reality.

In addition to feelings of depression, boomers are also beginning to experience feelings of envy. According to Jane Ciabattari, author of *Winning Moves,* such feelings are surfacing because "the Baby Boom is moving into midlife, a phase when limits begin to surface." She stated that as disappointment grows, "social conditions are ripe for a destructive epidemic of envy."[57]

Notice the subtle shift in thinking that stimulated that emotion. The parents of baby boomers growing up during the depression said, "You *can't* have everything." Baby boomers growing up in the 1960s and 1970s came to believe that "you *can* have everything." And by the 1980s, as the concept of entitlement flourished, this generation began to believe the credo "You *should* have everything."[58] The formula is simple: take one part heightened expectations, mix with the psychology of entitlement, place in a climate of lowered expectations, and the result is envy.

Psychologist Harriet Braiker said, "The country's obsession with money and greed breeds envy. I see it constantly." Here are just a few examples she has seen: husbands and wives envy each other's career successes, companies pit one employee against another to increase productivity, childless women envy other women's children.[59]

Often the emotion surfaces when we find that someone else is living out our dream of a successful and productive life. Ann Ulanov, coauthor of *Cinderella and Her Sisters: The Envied and the Envying,* said, "Those of us who as adults do not find a way to be true to who or what we are, what gives us our own identity, are also vulnerable. The self we refuse to live revenges itself, turns on us and makes us miserable. Then we envy people who are really living themselves."[60]

When you hear about someone five years younger than you becoming a millionaire or receiving a large pay raise, you feel a twinge. It isn't so much that you want what that person has achieved. Rather, it is a reminder that you may not be living up to your own dreams. Those feelings of personal disappointment turn to envy.

Often the target of our envy is not the highly successful but those who live in proximity to us. Psychologist Nathan Schwartz-Salant says, "People envy what is close to them, not what is distant." For example, "Someone who doesn't have money is not going to envy the Rockefellers. He's going to envy the guy next door who makes $100 more a week."[61]

Those who are envied find themselves ostracized because of their achievements. There is, after all, that traditional taboo about outdoing one's neighbors. It's OK to "keep up with the Joneses," but it is improper to outdo the Joneses. According to Garrison Keillor, it is almost as if a Greek chorus can be heard in the small towns chanting, "Who do you think you are? You're not so smart. . . . You're from Lake Wobegon. You shouldn't think *you're* somebody. You're no better than the rest of us."[62]

Just as depression should be avoided, so should envy. This powerful emotion can have a corrosive effect both on the individual and society. Personal energy is diverted into baser emotions. Initiative and creativity are criticized rather than emulated. Envy within a culture of entitlement breeds distrust, criticism, and mediocrity. Moreover, it further destroys the sense of community that has been lost in this society and desperately needs to be regained by the baby boom generation as it enters the years of midlife reevaluation and reexamination.

As this generation matures, it is in the midst of reevaluating its priorities. Changing personal goals requires a reevaluation, and changing social and economic realities requires a reexamination. As this generation evaluates its priorities, it does so in a cultural climate that complicates that assessment. Time is at a premium while choices are expanding. And many who have tasted the bitter fruit of disillusionment are changing their priorities and seeking the simple life.

NOTES

1. Kevin Leman, *The Birth Order Book* (Old Tappan, N.J.: Revell, 1985).
2. Paul Light, *Baby Boomers* (New York: Norton, 1988), 79.
3. Statistics from *Monitor Magazine*, June 1989, using data from the Census Bureau's 1988 Current Population Survey.
4. Light, *Baby Boomers*, 21.
5. Between yuppies and yuffies, some social commentators have defined another group known as "new collars." These twenty-five million baby boomers (nearly 33 percent) meet at least two criteria. They have at least a year of college and earn incomes between $20,000 and $40,000.
6. Patricia Friedman, "Yuffies: A Study in Failure," *Dallas Times Herald*, 26 February 1989, F-1.
7. Ibid., F-5.
8. *U.S. News and World Report*, 10 March 1986, 61.
9. *The Public Pulse*, May 1989.
10. News release, "Spiegel, Inc. Conducts Nationwide Survey Exploring Fantasy and the American Home," cited in *Research Alert*, 17 August 1990, 4.
11. Phillip Longman, *Born to Pay: The New Politics of Aging in America* (Boston: Houghton Mifflin, 1987), 38.
12. U.S. Census Bureau, *Historical Statistics*.
13. Kenneth T. Jackson, *The Crabgrass Frontier: The Suburbanization of the United States* (New York: Oxford Univ., 1985), 234.
14. Landon Jones, *Great Expectations: America and the Baby Boom Generation* (New York: Ballantine, 1980), 272.
15. U.S. Census Bureau, Current Population Reports, *Household and Family Characteristics: March 1978* (Washington, D.C.: U.S. Government Printing Office, series P-20, no. 340, 1979).
16. Longman, *Born to Pay*, 47.
17. William F. McKenna and Carla A. Hills, *The Report of the President's Commission on Housing*, 1982.
18. Longman, *Born to Pay*, 52.
19. J. Fred Geirtz and A. James Heins, "Real Estate: The Legacy of Tax Advantage," *Illinois Business Review*, June 1984.
20. A 1982 Louis Harris survey of recent home buyers showed that 40 percent bought houses for "investment purposes" and 25 percent for "tax reasons." Only 4 percent agreed with the reason "Want to own my own home, don't want to pay somebody rent." Louis Harris & Associates, *Buying a Home in the 80s: A Poll of American Attitudes* (Washington, D.C.: Federal National Mortgage Association, 1982), 17.
21. Anthony Downs, *The Revolution in Real Estate Finance* (Washington, D.C.: Brookings Institution, 1985), table 11, 17.
22. Jones, *Great Expectations*, 276.
23. Cynthia Crossen, "Poor Baby Boomers: They're Stuck with Real Estate," *The Wall Street Journal*, 10 July 1990, A-1.
24. Frank S. Levy and Richard C. Michel, "The Economic Future of the Baby Boom," paper delivered at the first annual conference of American for Generational Equity, Washington, D.C., 10 April 1986. Levittown prices from Jackson, *Crabgrass Frontier*, 236.
25. "First Home Shut Out," *Research Alert*, 30 March 1990, 4.

26. Ibid.

27. Harvard University Joint Center for Housing Studies, "The State of the Nation's Housing 1990," cited in *The Numbers News*, September 1990.

28. Harvard University Joint Center for Housing Studies, cited in "Home = Financial Security," *Research Alert*, 17 August 1990, 3.

29. Joint Economic Committee of Congress cited in *Research Alert*, 22 December 1989.

30. Walter Kiechel, "Two-Income Families Will Reshape the Consumer Markets," 10 March 1980.

31. Notice this comparison between family incomes (adjusted for inflation) in 1973 and 1983. In 1983, a couple with a household head aged twenty-five to thirty-four where both husband and wife worked had a combined median income only $3,400 higher than the amount a young couple had in 1973 by living on the husband's salary alone. U.S. Bureau of Census, Current Population Reports, *Projections of the Population of the United States, 1982 to 2080*.

32. Jane Bryant Quinn, "The Stalled Career," *Newsweek*, 29 November 1982, 19.

33. Quoted in Kara Kunkel, "Where Are Salaries Headed?" *Dallas Times Herald*, 24 September 1990, B-1.

34. The first person to coin the phrase appears to be Pauline Rose Clance, *The Imposter Phenomenon: Overcoming the Fear That Haunts Your Success* (Atlanta: Peachtree, 1985).

35. Laurence Shames, *The Hunger for More* (New York: Times Books, 1989), 128.

36. Joan Harvey, *If I'm So Successful, Why Do I Feel Like a Fake: The Imposter Phenomenon* (New York: St. Martin's, 1985).

37. Ross Goldstein, "The Imposter Syndrome," *The Boomer Report*, 15 July 1990.

38. Daniel Yankelovich, *The New Morality: A Profile of American Youth* (New York: McGraw Hill, 1974).

39. Daniel Yankelovich, "Work Values and the New Breed," in *Work in America*, ed. Clark Kerr and Jerome Rosow (New York: Van Nostran Reinhold, 1979).

40. "As of 1953, 58 percent of American households were clustered in the great economic middle taking in between $3,000 and $10,000 of after-tax earnings," Shames, *The Hunger*, 55.

41. Figures from "The Changing American Market," from a series of articles done by *Fortune* in 1953-1954, cited in Shames, *The Hunger*, 55.

42. David Bloom, quoted in "U.S. Rich and Poor Increase in Numbers; Middle Loses Ground," *Wall Street Journal*, 22 September 1986, 1.

43. John Koten, "The Shattered Middle Class: A Once Tightly Knit Middle Class Finds Itself Divided and Uncertain," *The Wall Street Journal*, 9 March 1987, 23.

44. Beth Brophy, "Middle-Class Squeeze," *U.S. News and World Report*, 18 August 1986, 36.

45. Jane Ciabattari, "Will the 90s Be the Age of Envy?" *Psychology Today*, December 1989, 48.

46. Dan Sperling, "A World View on the Baby Boomer Blues," *USA Today*, 21 April 1989.

47. Dr. Klerman found higher rates of depression in industrialized countries demonstrating that family ties tend to be weaker due to urbanization. Broken families (due to high rates of divorce and loosening family ties) were also a factor.

48. "Baby Boomer Blues," *First Magazine*, 30 July 1990, 36.
49. Ibid.
50. Kay Ebeling, "The Failure of Feminism," *Newsweek*, 19 November 1990, 9.
51. Claudia Wallis, "Onward, Women!" *Time*, 4 December 1989, 81.
52. Ibid., 86.
53. Jon I. Isenberg, "The Ulcer Updated," *Town and Country*, November 1986, 178.
54. "Being Down Is on the Rise," *Psychology Today*, October 1988, 54.
55. Martin Seligman, "Boomer Blues," *Psychology Today*, October 1988, 50.
56. Ibid., 52.
57. Ciabattari, "Will the 90s Be the Age?" 48.
58. Ibid.
59. Ibid.
60. Ibid., 49.
61. Ibid., 49.
62. Ibid., 50.

CHAPTER SIX
THE CRISIS OF PRIORITIES

John and Kay live life in the fast lane. When they aren't hard at work, they are hard at play. Anytime you run into them, it seems, they are rushing from one activity to another. They seem to be trying to cram as much into life as possible.

Yet their busyness isn't as blessed as it might seem. John is a successful salesman, and Kay runs her own florist shop. They have lots of money and are always ready to find ways to spend their disposable income. They have developed a lifestyle of affluence and opportunity. But sometimes they seem to have lost control of that lifestyle. It seems to be running them, rather than the other way around. Although they pushed their lifestyle to the limit in the 1980s, John and Kay are now spending more and more of their free time (when they can find free time) reevaluating the choices they have made and the priorities they have established.

The fast-paced lifestyle of many baby boomers springs from one philosophical foundation and two crushing realities. The philosophy is best expressed by a beer commercial, appropriately enough, which proclaims that "you can have it all." Boomers seeking the good life chased life experience after life experience in a frequently feeble attempt to have it all.

But the philosophy that feeds this frenetic, fast-paced life-style runs straight into two inexorable barriers of modern life: too many choices and too little time. A generation trying to have it all faces a growing crisis of priorities.

TRYING TO HAVE IT ALL

As we have noted, baby boomers grew up in a time of un-precedented affluence, optimism, and undiminished expecta-tions. Their formative years were filled with new experiences, new appliances, and new opportunities. Unlike their Depression-era parents, who learned to survive in bleak times, baby boomers were born into a world that almost seemed to be waiting for them to arrive.

The television industry was ready to inform and entertain at the mere flick of a switch. The consumer market was ready to sell them products and services that would meet their nearly insatia-ble demands for new experiences and personal fulfillment. In the dynamic economy of the fifties and sixties, there were always new products, new programs, and new opportunities. Boomers rarely had time for boredom to set in, for they were quickly off to a new experience and a new opportunity.

They were born into a world ripe for the plucking. A chosen generation, they raced toward a promised land flowing with en-tertainment and experience. Abstinence and moderation were not the bywords of this generation; hedonism and narcissism were.

Their world was typified by affluence, optimism, and oppor-tunity. Hedonism was in vogue by the early 1960s, so they pur-sued pleasure with headlong abandon. Impetuous and impatient, boomers developed what sociologists would later describe as a "psychology of entitlement." What previous generations saw as privileges, this generation saw as rights.

The year 1964 was a pivotal one, both demographically and economically. It was demographically important because it was the year when the first baby boomers turned eighteen—a magical year in the rite of passage—and the youngest baby boomers were born. But economically it was even more important. By 1964, American prosperity had reached such heights that, for the first time in any nation ever, urban Americans were able to pay for the necessities of food, clothing, and shelter with less than half their aggregate after-tax income.[1] Fifty-two cents of every earned dollar were available for luxuries rather than necessities. What had been a privileged purchase for others became consumer rights for baby boomers and their parents.

That unprecedented amount of disposable income not only purchased appliances, stereos, and color TVs for Mom and Dad; it was also used to send middle-class kids to college with sometimes even enough left over for a high school student to buy the newly introduced Ford Mustang. But its most significant impact was on the psychology of consumer behavior. Now,

> there was, rather suddenly, enough money so that *and* rather than *or* became the operative notion in American spending; this was new. People could fix up the house *and* have a Florida vacation *and* move up from a Pontiac to an Oldsmobile. Freedom of choice was phasing over into freedom from having to choose; "having it all" was just beyond the frontier's next range of ups and downs.[2]

But in the 1970s and 1980s, many baby boomers discovered that there were limits to their pursuit of the good life. In addition to the realities of too many choices and too little time, many in this generation found that they did not have the financial resources to realize many of their dreams. In answer to the question, Why can't I have it all? columnist George Will replied, "Reality, that's why."

> This is the saddest story ever told. A whole generation believed the Michelob beer commercial and, consequently, got its heart broken. Many baby boomers expected a pot of gold but have settled for a Dove Bar. . . . A *Wall Street Journal* report on "strapped yuppies" quotes one such: "We can't afford houses and cars, but we'll spend $2 on a Dove Bar so we can try to tell ourselves we aren't doing as badly as our pocketbooks say we are." A Dove Bar is ice cream. It is a flimsy prop for self-esteem. Many baby boomers are big spenders, but often their foreign travel, pricey audio systems, and gourmet mustards are compensatory consumption.[3]

Those who could afford all that life could provide were ceremoniously dubbed "yuppies." A cover article on "Yuppies" in *Newsweek*, which appeared shortly after their coronation, identified a new state of consciousness. The editors called the state "Transcendental Acquisition, in which the perfection of their possessions enables them to rise above the messy turmoil of their emotional lives."[4] Yuppies, they said, live to buy. Yuppies bought the idea and therefore tried to prove that you can indeed have it all.

For yuppies, having it all usually meant expensive, exclusive, and top of the line.

> The name of the game is best. Buying it, owning it, using it, eating it, wearing it, growing it, driving it, doing whatever with it. Yuppies are said to have insatiable appetites for designer clothes, computers, video recorders, pasta makers, phone-answering devices, espresso machines, pagers, and other gadgets. Volvos and BMWs are very popular. An Atlanta auto dealer reports that young adults fill a waiting list of up to 60 days for $32,500 Jaguars.[5]

But having it all wasn't always as glamorous as it might have seemed. Many professionals found themselves trapped in a gilded cage of their own making. The conspicuous consumption of the upwardly mobile was, like the compensatory consumption of the downwardly mobile, also tied to self-esteem.

> This, according to *The New York Times*, was the dilemma of a certain group of financial professionals who had "sort of reduced [them]selves to an equation where net worth equals self-worth," and who had bought into a lifestyle whose customs and demands were nearly as rigorous and expensive as life at a royal court. These people *had* to live in certain neighborhoods, *had* to send their children to certain schools, *had* to eat in certain restaurants, *had* to vacation on certain islands. Except by climbing to what was, by the brittle consensus of their own circle, the very pinnacle of the lifestyle pyramid, they had no way of determining how they were doing. They had no other standard of value; they had no other life.[6]

Turning the values of their parents on their heads, baby boomers found themselves judged not by what they saved but by what they spent. The core values of the Protestant work ethic, such as savings and sacrifice, were replaced by the materialistic values of spending and self-assertion.

Although that was an eighties phenomenon, it was identified in the seventies by Charles Reich in *The Greening of America*. He called it "impoverishment by substitution." Our consumer society, according to Reich, withheld basic needs such as a sense of purpose or a sense of community and offered in their place material goods that could be purchased.

Shopping became one of the most popular endeavors of both young and old. When asked what their favorite activity was, 93 percent of teenage girls chose store-hopping over such items as dating, exercising, or even going to the movies.[7] Newsmagazines in the early 1980s even identified "compulsive shopping" as a psychological disorder, a diagnosis that gained clinical respectability by the middle of that decade. Compulsive shopping, said one writer, "was the flip side of money addiction—a dysfunction, so to speak, of the output mode rather than the input mode."[8]

Throughout the 1980s, people were buying new products in unprecedented ways. Microwaves were in only 27 percent of American households in 1982 but were in nearly two-thirds by 1987. At the beginning of the decade, VCRs were almost nonexistent. By 1986, half of American families owned one. And even though 99 percent of this country's homes already had televisions, 25 percent purchased a new one in 1986.[9]

The spending binge was both extensive and diverse as economist Robert J. Samuelson documented in his column in *Newsweek:*

> If you take an inventory of what Americans have bought in the past six years (1983-1988), your list will include 62 million microwave ovens, 57 million washers and dryers, 88 million cars and light trucks, 105 million color-television sets, 46 million refrigerators and freezers, 63 million VCR's, 31 million cordless phones and 30 million telephone-answering machines. There's a message in these numbers. In the 1980s Americans went on a spending spree unlike anything since the late 1940s.[10]

But not only was this boom in consumerism a boom in hedonism; it was also a bull market for narcissism. Turning John Kennedy's dictum on its head, baby boomers were asking what the country and the culture could do for them. Even more important, they were seeing what they could do for themselves.

Instead of joining a Peace Corps or Vista, they were on a fast track toward self-improvement. They were jogging, playing tennis, and working out in health clubs. They were learning how to cook with a wok or how to program a computer. And best-selling books with such titles as *I'm OK—You're OK* and *Looking Out for Number One* illustrated baby boomers' consuming interest with self and self-improvement.

Trading a Woodstock mind-set for a Sharper Image mind-set might seem like a dramatic shift, and perhaps it was. In part it was trading youthful, university world idealism for thirty-something, business world pragmatism. In part, it may have been a willingness to trade "changing the world" for "changing oneself." But for many, the withdrawal into self may have merely been a way to compensate for disappointment.

As baby boomers reach midlife, they are beginning to bump into the limits of their fervent dash for pleasure and self-expression. If not limited by family, career, or finances, boomers are still finding that they must choose and establish priorities because there are simply too many choices and too little time.

PLURALISM: TOO MANY CHOICES

The baby boom generation is confronted with more choices than any other generation in history. Think of the possible choices of furniture, houses, cars, television sets, television programs and, yes, even choices of philosophies and religions. A generation that demanded freedom to choose now faces a bewildering array of options that leads to the burnout of overchoice.

When Henry Ford produced his Model Ts earlier in this century, they came in one color: basic black. But changes in production have given consumers choices the car buyers in Henry Ford's day could not have imagined.

> When the assembly line was created at the turn of the century, it was profitable to paint every Ford black. In the 1950s, changes in manufacturing technology made it just as profitable to paint cars every color of the rainbow. Automation—later abetted by the computer—opened an enormous market for customization, personalization and individual choice. Even blue jeans are no longer all blue; they come in dozens of colors and hundreds of varieties. If you include optional equipment, colors and models, you can now buy any of several million "unique" cars. To tap this market, advertising has inflated—indeed exalted

—individual choice. The deciding, choosing, hedonistically pre-occupied individual has become a profitable target.[11]

CONSUMER CHOICES: A RECORD NUMBER

A record 13,244 consumer products were introduced in 1990,[12] and many consumers are overwhelmed by the growing problem of overchoice. The average grocery store carries 17,901 items, up from 7,800 in 1970. Shoppers are often overwhelmed by the variety of sizes, shapes, and colors of products ranging from toilet paper to aspirin.

Below are the number of new products introduced in 1990 by product category:

Products Category	Introduced
Baby foods	31
Beverages	1,143
Breakfast cereals	123
Condiments	2,028
Pet food	130
Health, beauty aids	2,379
Tobacco	31

Those figures don't even include choices proliferating in cars (656 if you include all the versions of every make) or in mutual funds (2,718 stock and bond mutual funds) or in television channels (at least 70 different national cable networks).

Consumer choice just a few decades ago usually consisted of three models of appliance: good, better, and best. Today consumers can easily become overwhelmed by the number of styles, colors, and options on such things as VCRs, stereos, telephones, televisions, and cars.

Nevertheless, consumer choices proliferate as companies attempt to fill every marketing niche possible with their broad range of products.

The range of acceptable tastes in the late 1950s was so narrow, in fact, that Hart Schaffner & Marx prospered in men's tailored clothing despite offering only three styles of suits in its best lines. But today the range is much wider and many companies can't succeed unless they offer a broad choice. While Chrysler

Corp. sold 10 basic car models in 1965, today its dealers stock 25 models. Coca-Cola has gone from a single product to what its maker now calls an "umbrella brand," with permutations that include Coca-Cola Classic and Diet Cherry Coke, each aimed at a different type of consumer. Hartmarx has expanded the three basic suit styles in its Hart Schaffner & Marx line to 15. And Levi Strauss & Co., which produced one uniform for an entire generation, now sells more than 5,000 styles of apparel.[13]

Choice in the service industry is no less difficult. Finding a place to eat that pleases the whole family may well be next to impossible. And choosing doctors, dentists, therapists, mechanics, gardeners, and so on can be equally taxing.

Yet the multiplication of consumer options pales when compared to the pluralization that has taken place in Western society. Choices and opportunities in philosophies, religions, and lifestyles have increased dramatically in the last few decades.

In previous centuries, a Judeo-Christian worldview provided a cohesive unit of culture. But in the twentieth century a Judeo-Christian consensus eroded and the pluralization of worldviews increased.

By the time the baby boom generation reached adolescence, it claimed freedom to "do its own thing." It did not look to the adult community and traditional values for guidance. Instead, it turned to the generation it trusted the most: its own. Free from the constraints of parental authority and cultural mores, baby boomers made up their own rules as they went. They determined what was fashionable and constructed their own lifestyles and life philosophies. By the end of the 1960s, pluralism was in full bloom.

The impact on society has been significant. First, according to sociologist Os Guinness, the increase in choice and change leads to a decrease in commitment and continuity.[14] If someone lost a silk handkerchief inherited from his Victorian great-grandfather, he would search for it diligently. But no one would bother to hunt for a lost paper tissue. Commitment and continuity are foreign to the notion of the paper handkerchief.

Likewise, in a world brimming with options, commitment to a viewpoint or lifestyle often resembles the commitment to a tissue. A nagging concern is, What if the lifestyle or worldview I have chosen is wrong, or at least wrong for me? Commitment, therefore, in this generation is rare. Just as tissue is disposable, so are lifestyles, values, beliefs, relationships. Even marriages have become disposable, thus making it no surprise that baby boomers have a higher divorce rate than any preceding generation.

A second effect of pluralization is a high degree of self-consciousness.[15]

> Each choice raises questions. Might they? Could they? Should they? Will they? Won't they? What if they had? What if they hadn't? And so on. The forest of choices raised by modern options leads deeper and deeper into the dark freedom, then the even darker anxiety, of seemingly infinite possibility.
>
> Like a hall of mirrors, the reflections recede forever. Choice is no longer simple. Choosing is never complete. The outside world becomes more questionable, the inside world more complex. What can they believe? What ought they to do? Who are they? Modern people are constant question marks to each other. Permanent self-consciousness is the price of modern choice.[16]

The self becomes a prime fixation as each individual asks, What do *I* want? Will this choice please *me?* Ultimately, the self became deified.

Third, pluralization makes this generation conversion-prone.[17] Faced with so many options, many boomers attempted to sample all that life can offer. Serial conversion and reconversion to a variety of beliefs and philosophies reached its apex in the 1960s. For example, Jerry Rubin, a pioneer in spiritual witchcraft, claimed to have experienced eighteen different "trips" in five years, including such things as est, Gestalt therapy, bioenergetics, meditation, and sex therapy.[18]

Boomers in the nineties are still conversion-prone but commitment shy. Burned by previous commitments and convictions, this generation is less enthusiastic about converting than it was in its early years. But boomers are still cycling through beliefs and lifestyles at an unprecedented rate. They flock to self-improvement seminars the way they once did to rock concerts. They follow trends, fads, and fashions as religiously as before. And as boomers enter midlife (a stage known for its significant changes and conversions), who can predict what this generation will do?

Not only are boomers having difficulty with priorities because there are too many choices; they also have too little time.

THE NINETIES' TIME CRUNCH

It has, perhaps, always been true that "time is money." But for the baby boom generation, that maxim has taken a new twist. In the frenetic nineties, time has become even more scarce than money and, therefore, more valuable. As with any commodity, the law of supply and demand determines value. In the last two decades, free time has grown scarce and hence has become a precious possession.

The 1990s are the decade of the time famine. Leisure time, once plentiful and elastic, is now scarce and elusive. A generation seeking the good life is finding it increasingly difficult to enjoy it, even if it can afford it. What money was in the 1980s, time has become in the 1990s.

The crunch was already developing in the 1980s. One writer, celebrating the "Year of the Yuppie," cautioned, "Despite all the preoccupation with material goods, time can be the overachiever's most precious possession."[19] Laurence Shames stated:

> The war between lifestyle and life . . . often boiled down to the conflict between money and time. There simply weren't enough hours in the day to earn a living *and* go to the health club *and* do the shopping *and* eat the mahi-mahi *and* dabble in the kitchen or the workshop or at the keyboard or the easel. Something had to go.[20]

According to a Lou Harris survey, the amount of leisure time enjoyed by the average American has shrunk 37 percent since 1973. A major reason is the expanding work week. In the same period, the average work week (including time spent commuting) had increased from less than 41 hours to nearly 47 hours.[21] And in many professions, such as medicine, law, and accounting, an eighty-hour week is not uncommon. Harris, therefore, concludes that "Time may have become the most precious commodity in the land."[22]

AN UNEXPECTED TURN

Our current time crunch caught most people off-guard. Optimistic futurists in the 1950s and 1960s, with visions of utopia dancing in their heads, predicted ample hours of leisure. If there was a crisis ahead, it was what Americans at the turn of the century were going to do with all their free time. Computers, satellites, and robotics would remove the menial aspects of labor and deliver abundant opportunities for rest and recreation. At the time, their predictions seemed to have ample support.

The number of hours of leisure increased dramatically in the first half of the twentieth century. The average employed American in 1959 had fully twenty more nonworking hours per week than a worker in 1900 had. Not counting time spent sleeping, the typical worker had roughly 3,700 leisure hours a year,[23] and that number seemed to be increasing. Testimony before a Senate subcommittee in 1967 predicted that "by 1985, people could be working just 22 hours a week or 27 weeks a year or could retire at 38."[24]

Well, computers crunch data at unimaginable speeds, orbiting satellites cover the globe with a dizzying array of messages, and robots zap together everything from cars to computer chips at speeds far exceeding their human counterparts. Yet those and other technological feats have not freed Americans from their labor. Most people are busier today than ever.

Instead of being the average worker's friend, technology has become more of an enemy. "Technology is increasing the heartbeat," says Manhattan architect James Trunzo, who designs automated environments. "We are inundated with information. The mind can't handle it all. The pace is so fast now, I sometimes feel like a gunfighter dodging bullets."[25]

Actually technology isn't the problem as much as the heightened expectations engendered by it. Increased speed and efficiency programmed into appliances, computers, and other technology have made it possible to accomplish much more than in previous decades. But that efficiency has also fostered a desire to take on additional responsibilities and thereby squeeze even more activities into already crammed calendars.

Urbanization has also increased the pace of life, thus contributing to our feeling of busyness. One researcher in a large-scale "City-Town" project observed the speed and behavior of children in typical city supermarkets and town grocery stores. An average city child walked nearly twice as fast through a supermarket as his small town counterpart, and the town child spent three times as much time with clerks and other shoppers than did his urban counterpart.[26]

Researchers also found faster walking speeds in Boston than in the less populous town of Concord, Massachusetts.[27] Other researchers reported faster walking speeds in cities such as Philadelphia and New York when compared to small and moderate-sized towns.[28]

As the pace has increased, overcommitment and busyness have been elevated to socially desirable standards. Being busy is chic and trendy. Pity the poor person with an organized life and a livable schedule.

It's little wonder that most of the products now being developed are not time savers but time controllers. In the 1950s when a cornucopia of appliances was being developed, most were designed to save time and remove drudgery from housework (such as vacuum cleaners, dishwashers, mixers). By comparison, most of the products developed in the 1980s were time controllers (VCRs, answering machines, automatic teller machines). The new devices don't really save time, but they do allow a harried consumer to control his or her use of that time more effectively.

Technological efficiency has also increased competition. Labor-saving devices that were supposed to make life easier frequently force people to work harder. Baby boomers who are competing intensely with one another for jobs and prestigious promotions voraciously employ the latest technology to give them an edge. Faxes, LANs, car phones, and laptop computers are viewed as necessities if one is to remain competitive.

But technology isn't enough. So most professionals, especially in service industries (law, accounting, advertising), work long hours and frequent weekends in an effort to meet their clients' seemingly endless needs and demands.

The work ethic seems out of control. In the frenetic dash for competitiveness or just plain survival, leisure time becomes a scarce commodity. "My wife and I were sitting on the beach in Anguilla on one of our rare vacations," recalls architect Trunzo, "and even there my staff was able to reach me. There are times when our lives are clearly leading us."[29]

TIME AND LIFESTYLE CHANGES

The time crunch has made baby boomers an impatient bunch. They demand, and frequently receive, flexibility. First, they are demanding flexibility in their schedules. Flextime is but one concession given to many in the workplace. Employers are finding that rigid schedules are less attractive to key employees who want greater control over their hours at work.

A growth industry in the 1990s is home offices. Computers, faxes, and home copiers are making it possible for many to work out of their homes and thereby gain additional flexibility.

Second, this generation not only demands flexibility in the workplace; it demands it in the marketplace as well. Busy boomers can only spend their money in stores that are open. To meet the demand, ATMs (automatic teller machines) dispense money twenty-four hours a day, 365 days a year. Most grocery stores are open around the clock. And department stores and service industries find that they must be open seven days a week to be competitive.

Boomer busyness has led to a revitalization of catalog sales. Originally the staple of rural consumers, catalogs have proliferated because they provide information and save time. "For one thing [direct mail] provides lots of information, which baby boomers crave. . . . Time is a key factor here, as well; they like being able to order 24 hours a day, on their schedule. A catalog linked to a 24-hour, toll-free number can be the ideal way to reach out and touch a Yuppie; just ask L. L. Bean."[30]

Yet the greatest lifestyle change has been not the need to cope with these time pressures but rather the desire to reject them for a simpler lifestyle. Many boomers are saying good-bye to materialism in search of a simpler and more meaningful lifestyle. Bicycles, board games, and macaroni and cheese may not seem like the beginning of a revolution. Nevertheless, social commentators are noting the latest trend to return to basics and to simplify lifestyles.

> After a 10-year bender of gaudy dreams and godless consumerism, Americans are starting to trade down. They want to reduce their attachments to status symbols, fast-track careers and great expectations of Having It All. Upscale is out; downscale is in. . . . In place of materialism, many Americans are embracing simpler pleasures and homier values.[31]

Many baby boomers are trading disposable, expensive, and high tech for recyclable, cheap, and nostalgic. Although the move to the simpler life is still a minority, it reflects this generation's concern with priorities and lifestyle. Only a fraction have slowed down to date, but a clear majority want to slow down. In a Time/CNN poll of five hundred adults, 69 percent said they would like to "slow down and live a more relaxed life," whereas only 19 percent said they would like to "live a more exciting, faster-paced life."[32]

Family is one of the major reasons many boomers want to slow down. Time pressures are destroying the American family. Families are often overscheduled and overcommitted. And when parents are preoccupied, children and family relationships are neglected.

TIME AND THE FAMILY

A recent survey by Cynthia Langham at the University of Detroit found that parents and children spend only 14.5 minutes per day talking to each other.[33] That's less time than a quarter of football and certainly much less time than most people spend commuting to work. She says that many people are shocked to hear the 14.5 minutes statistic. But once they take a stopwatch to their conversations, they realize that she is right.

Tragically, that 14.5-minute statistic is actually misleading since most of that time is squandered on chitchat such as, "What's for supper?" and, "Have you finished your homework?" True, meaningful communication between parent and child unfortunately occupies only about two minutes each day. Langham concludes, "Nothing indicates that parent-child communications are improving. If things are changing, it's for the worse."[34]

She points to two major reasons for this breakdown. First is the change in the work force. A few decades ago the dinner table was a forum for family business and communication. But now, Dad's still at work, Mom is headed for a business meeting, and Sister has to eat and run to make it to her part-time job. Even when everyone is home, there are constant interruptions to meaningful communication.

The greatest interruption is the second reason for poor parent-child communication: television. Urie Bronfenbrenner of Cornell has reported a forty-year decline in the amount of time children spend with their parents, much of the recent loss due to television.[35] TV sabotages much of the already limited time families spend together. Meals are frequently eaten in front of the "electronic fireplace." After dinner, talk-starved families gather to watch shows that, ironically, portray congenial families with good communication skills, such as the Huxtables on "The Cosby Show." When TV programs deal with issues families might discuss (honesty, drugs, pregnancy), few families take advantage of the opportunities to talk about the dilemma and provide moral instruction.

The greeting card business has developed a whole new product line for busy parents. More and more children are finding cards in their backpacks that proclaim "Have a good day at school" or under their pillows that lament "I wish I were there to tuck you in."

And little wonder. A 1989 survey done by *Family Circle* documented the loss of time, especially for working mothers. The article titled "Never Enough Time?" began, "Remember 'quality time'? In the 1980's that was what you sandwiched in for the children between the office and the housework. We all learned how valuable time was in the school of hard knocks. Life was what happened while we were busy making other plans, to paraphrase ex-Beatle John Lennon. That was then."[36]

A resounding 71 percent of those surveyed said their lives had gotten busier in the previous year.[37] Nearly a third cited these reasons for their hectic lives: increased work load at the office, the demands of a new job, starting a business, or returning to work. Not only were the women working longer hours (40%) but many were also working on weekends (38%), and nearly a third often took work home.[38]

Dual income couples reported major difficulties finding time for each other. Negotiating schedules and juggling calendars were daily activities. Three out of four women in the survey reported that finding enough time to be alone with their husbands is "often" (22%) or "sometimes" (53%) a major stress in their relationships.[39] When asked, "In a time crunch, who gets put on the back burner?" half (50%) said friends, then husbands (25%), and then other family members (12%).

Some of the hardest hit by time pressures were single parents. One single mother with two teenagers in Illinois writes: "I am responsible for a house and yard, work 40 hours a week, take college classes, run a local support group for divorced and widowed women and am involved with a retreat group through church. I have time because I *make* time."[40]

But whether they were in the work force or were full-time homemakers, more than half (56%) of women were either "very" or "somewhat" dissatisfied with the amount of time they have alone.[41] Only 30 percent try to set aside four or more hours a week just for themselves. Another 30 percent carve out two to three hours. But 19 percent say they give themselves an hour or less a week, and 20 percent do not allot themselves any leisure time at all.[42]

The effects of time pressures on the family have been devastating. Yale psychology professor Edward Ziglar somberly warned, "As a society, we're at the breaking point as far as family is concerned."[43] Homemaking and child rearing are full-time activities. But when both husband and wife work, maintaining a home and rearing a family become extremely difficult. In the increasing numbers of single-parent households, the task becomes next to impossible.

Someone has to drive the carpool, make lunches, do laundry, cope with sick kids and broken appliances, and pay the bills. In progressive households, household tasks are shared as the traditional husband/wife division of labor begins to break down. In others, super-Mom is expected to step into the gap and perform indefatigably.

Inevitably, children are forced to grow up quickly and take on responsibilities they should never be forced to shoulder. Some children are effectively abandoned—if not physically, emotionally—and must grow up on their own. Others are latch-key kids who are forced to mature emotionally beyond their years. The demands take their toll and create what sociologist David Elkind called the "hurried child" syndrome.[44]

But even children who are the focus of their parents' attention feel time pressures—perhaps more so. Soccer practices, ballet lessons, piano recitals, and karate classes fill up young children's social schedules. Frequently their lives rival the complexity of their parents', and time for play, reflection, or just plain "goofing off" gets squeezed out in a blur of activities.

Allan Carlson of the Rockford Institute said, "It may be that the same loss of leisure among parents produces this pressure for rapid achievement and overprogramming of children."[45] When time is scarce and careers are all-important, parents frequently turn the parenting process into a business venture. Parents invest their scarce commodity of time into their children and expect a generous return on investment. Not surprisingly, the August 1989 issue of *Atlantic Monthly* carried an article aptly titled "Kids As Capital."[46] In the end, children become products to be developed and improved rather than individuals to be loved and nurtured.

Thus is the legacy of a generation with too many choices and too little time. It remains to be seen how boomers will order their priorities. But unless relationships are made a priority, they will suffer and inevitably lead to a crisis of relationships in this decade.

NOTES

1. "The Great Shopping Spree," *Time*, 8 January 1965, 59.
2. Laurence Shames, *The Hunger for More* (New York: Time Books, 1989), 35.
3. George Will, "Reality Says You Can't Have It All," *Newsweek*, 3 February 1986.
4. Jerry Adler et al., "The Year of the Yuppie," *Newsweek*, 31 December 1984, 19.
5. Steve Huntley, with Gail Bronson and Kenneth Walsh, "Yumpies, YAP's, Yuppies—Who They Are," *U.S. News and World Report*, 16 April 1984, 78.
6. Shames, *Hunger for More*, 167.
7. Myron Magnet, "The Money Society," *Fortune*, 6 July 1987, 26.
8. Shames, *Hunger for More*, 148.
9. Ibid., 93.
10. Robert J. Samuelson, "The Binge Is Over," *Newsweek*, 10 July 1989, 35.
11. Martin Seligman, "Boomer Blues," *Psychology Today*, October 1988, 52.
12. Kevin Maney, "Consumers Face Flood of Products," *USA Today*, 12 July 1991, B-1.
13. John Koten, "The Shattered Middle Class: Upheaval in Middle-Market Forces Changes in Selling Strategies," *Wall Street Journal*, 13 March 1987.
14. Os Guinness, *The Gravedigger File* (Downers Grove, Ill.: InterVarsity, 1983), 96.
15. Peter L. Berger, *The Heretical Imperative* (Garden City, N.Y.: Doubleday, 1961), chapter 1.
16. Guinness, *Gravedigger File*, 101–2.
17. Peter L. Berger, *The Precarious Vision* (Garden City, N.Y.: Doubleday, 1961), 17ff.
18. Christopher Lasch, *The Culture of Narcissism* (New York: Norton, 1979), 44.
19. Eric Gelman, "They Live to Buy," *Newsweek*, 31 December 1984, 28.
20. Shames, *Hunger for More*, 171–72.
21. Nancy Gibbs, "How America Has Run Out of Time," *Time*, 24 April 1989, 58.
22. Ibid.
23. Shames, *Hunger for More*, 211.
24. Ibid., 59.
25. Quoted in ibid.
26. H. F. Wright, "The City-Town Project: A Study of Children in Communities Differing in Size," cited in *The Social Psychology of Time* (Newbury Park, Calif.: Sage, 1988), 41.
27. S. Milgram, "The Experience of Living in Cities," *Science*, 167 (1970), 1461–68.
28. Cited in Milgram, "Living in Cities."
29. Ibid., 60.
30. Gelman, "They Live to Buy," 29.
31. Janice Castro, "The Simple Life," *Time*, 8 April 1991, 58.
32. Ibid.

33. Quoted in Leslie Barker, "We Never Seem to Talk Any More," *Dallas Morning News*, 25 September 1989, C-1.

34. Ibid.

35. Landon Jones, *Great Expectations: America and the Baby Boom Generation* (New York: Ballantine, 1980), 139.

36. Stephanie Abarbanel and Karen Peterson, "Never Enough Time? You Can Beat the Clock," *Family Circle*, 14 March 1989, 115.

37. Ibid., 116.

38. Ibid.

39. Ibid., 119.

40. Ibid., 136.

41. Ibid., 134.

42. Ibid.

43. Gibbs, "How America Has Run Out," 58.

44. David Elkin, *The Hurried Child* (Reading, Mass.: Addison-Wesley, 1981).

45. Gibbs, "How America Has Run Out," 64.

46. Jonathan Rauch, "Kids As Capital," *Atlantic Monthly*, August 1989, 56–61.

CHAPTER SEVEN

THE CRISIS OF RELATIONSHIPS

It seemed to Bob and Sally that all the rules about relationships had changed. When they decided to get married and start a family, they wanted a family like the ones in which they were reared. But they knew that times had changed, including their own circumstances.

Both Bob and Sally had been married before. Their parents never had to worry about divorce, child support, or stepchildren. This was a daily part of Bob and Sally's new life together. Both of them worked. Their parents never had to balance priorities and schedules in a two-career marriage. But now that they were starting a family of their own, they faced additional difficulties. Sally was an executive rising in the corporate structure. She worried that leaving the workplace during a tight economy might prevent her from ever returning. Sally faces conflicts each day as her career and family pull her in different directions while economic concerns nag at her psyche.

Bob and Sally's lives were complicated enough, but another complicating element would be added. Bob's father died a few years ago, leaving his feeble mother to fend for herself. Every holiday visit made it more apparent that she needed attention and supervision. Bob and Sally knew that soon Bob's mother would have to move in with them so that they could provide her with better care.

Building strong relationships within the family and community have always been difficult but never harder than in the current social climate. External factors seem to be conspiring against building meaningful and fulfilling relationships. Time constraints inhibit the development of deep relationships. Families rarely gather around the dinner table for lengthy and leisurely family discussions anymore. Children no longer sit at the foot of Grandpa's chair on the porch to listen to stories. Families are moving too fast to find the quality time necessary to build strong relationships.

Changing family structures complicate relationships. Divorce and remarriage shuffle family members together in foreign and awkward ways. Parents and children try to adapt to the changing circumstances as well as they can. But the new rules are difficult to discern and follow. The social norms of extended families and nuclear families have given way to blended families and what one commentator called "neo-nuclear" families.

Anticipating this possible confusion, one writer described the following scenario of a family gathering in the future:

> On a spring afternoon, half a century from today, the Joneses are gathered to sing "Happy Birthday" to Junior. There's Dad and his third wife, Mom and her second husband, Junior's two half brothers from his father's first marriage, his six stepsisters from his mother's spouse's previous unions, 100-year-old Great Grandpa, all eight of Junior's current "grandparents," assorted aunts, uncles-in-law and stepcousins. While one robot scoops up the gift wrappings and another blows out the candles, Junior makes a wish . . . that he didn't have so many relatives.[1]

Older baby boomers find themselves "sandwiched" between their parents and their children. Caught between the needs of their growing children and the needs of their aging parents, boomers are in the difficult position of trying to allocate scarce resources fairly, such as time and money. Frequently there is not enough of any resource to go around.

THE TURN INWARD

Strong relationships come from a strong commitment to family and community. Yet Americans have always been known—since colonial times—as rugged, self-reliant individualists. Though there have been times in which family and community have flourished, the latter decades of the twentieth century have not been such periods.

If anything, the baby boom generation has been more self-reliant and individualistic than previous generations. It is more committed to self than to family and community. Instead of reaching out, this generation has turned inward. And when boomers reach out, it is with the goal of finding relationships that meet their personal needs.

In *Habits of the Heart,* Robert Bellah expresses the contemporary pattern of relationships in this way: "The idea that people must take responsibility for deciding what they want and finding relationships that meet their needs is widespread. Individuals may want lasting relationships, but such relationships are possible only so long as they meet the needs of the two people involved."[2]

Relationships founded upon convenience and personal need? Relationships built upon self-actualization? The baby boom generation did not discover such relationships of convenience, but it has certainly elevated the concept to an art form. Defining relationships in terms of self-fulfillment has been one of the boom generation's innovations and explains (at least in part) why boomers encounter such a crisis of relationships.

Members of this generation grew up with heightened expectations but became discouraged in their youth and disillusioned in their adult years. They traded the secure affluence of their childhood for the insecurity of inflation, recession, and a stock market crash; the comfortable community of their youth for the anomie of mass society.

Confused and disoriented, they refused to look to the institutions they had repudiated during their adolescence—family, church, and community. Instead, they turned en masse in the only remaining direction: inward. Thomas Wolfe described the 1970s as the "Me Decade," and for good reason. As successive waves of baby boomers turned inward, they changed the nature of society and redefined the foundation of interpersonal relationships.

This generation gave birth to the human potential movement and provided fertile soil for the seeds that would come to be known as the New Age movement. They turned books such as *Passages* and *How to Be Your Own Best Friend* into best-sellers. And they popularized dozens of self-improvement cults and techniques. Throughout the 1970s and 1980s, baby boomers were the ones reading books, listening to tapes, and attending seminars—all with the goal of discovering and nurturing "the self." During that period, baby boomers were asked "which was more important, (a) working hard and doing what is expected of oneself, or (b) doing the things that give you personal satisfaction and pleasure"; two out of three chose pleasure over hard work.[3]

No wonder baby boomers frequently struggle with the idea of relationships rooted in duty and obligation. Foreign is the idea of friendship based upon self-denial and self-sacrifice. Relationships must be built on more than communication; they must also be built upon commitment. Unfortunately, baby boomers are rearing families in an era of disposable relationships. The lifelong commitment of marriage has given way to the idea of "open marriages" and now even "serial marriages" (a series of marriages to different people each who meets different needs at different life stages).

Those dramatic changes in social statistics have forced some commentators to begin talking about America as a "post-marital society."[4] Although that may be straining at hyperbole, there are certainly a number of marriage statistics that suggest that many in this generation consider marriage an optional lifestyle. The average age of first marriage has been rising, the number of never-married is up, and the number of unmarried, cohabiting couples is up.

FAMILY RELATIONSHIPS
MARRIAGE AND FAMILY

Though the boom generation may be redefining the nature of marriage, that does not mean that marriage and family are unimportant to it. On the contrary, marriage and family are still central, as numerous polls demonstrate.

The Roper Organization asked Americans what they believed constituted "the good life." The ranking was instructive. First was material aspirations; second was a happy marriage; and third was children.[5] A MassMutual study of family values showed that eight out of ten Americans reported that their families were the greatest source of pleasure in their lives—more than friends, religion, recreation, or work.[6] In a survey of ten thousand *Better Homes and Gardens* readers (a majority of which were baby boomers), more than half said their relationship to their spouse was the single most important factor in their personal happiness—well ahead of children, spiritual or religious belief, health, or even financial security.[7]

Whereas Americans may be enthusiastic about their own marriage and family, they are considerably less sanguine about *other* peoples' families. They apparently suffer from what might be called "a Lake Wobegon effect," where "all the women are strong, all the men are good-looking, and all the children are above average." In other words, *their* marriage is fine, but the rest of the marriages in this country are not.

Take, for example, the MassMutual Family Values Study. Whereas 81 percent pointed to their family as the greatest source of pleasure, a majority (56 percent) rated the quality of family in the U.S. "only fair" or "poor." Almost six in ten expected it to get *worse* in the next ten years, and 85 percent said that most people put a higher value on material things than on family. The survey concluded that "Americans seem to see the family in decline everywhere but in their own home."[8]

Similar results can be found in nearly every nationwide poll about attitudes toward marriage and family. A Gallup poll for a special edition of *Newsweek* on the twenty-first century family found that Americans believe that the family is worse off today than it was ten years ago. The same sample split evenly when asked if they thought the family would be better off or worse off in ten years.[9] When asked, Do you feel that family life in America is in trouble? eight out of ten *Better Homes and Gardens* readers answered with a resounding yes.[10]

That ambivalence about marriage is demonstrated not only in attitudes but in behavior. The number of Americans fitting into the Census Bureau category of "adults living alone" has been growing for decades. More and more adults are postponing marriage or foregoing the institution altogether. As one demographics expert in the 1980s accurately predicted, "In the 1990s, marriage will be an optional lifestyle" because "marriage is becoming less relevant to Americans."[11]

SINGLES AND LATE MARRIAGE

Although the institution of marriage shouldn't be put on the endangered species list, it nevertheless has become much less relevant to baby boomers. They have chosen the single life in much greater numbers than previous generations. Reversing the trend that brought their large numbers into existence, baby boomers marry later and less frequently. In fact, those two trends are actually interrelated. Frequently boomers' desire to postpone marriage reduces their chances of ever getting married. "Love and marriage used to go together like a horse and carriage. But today young people are postponing marriage for so long that an unprecedented number will never marry at all."[12]

Since the 1960s, the median age for a first marriage has risen to unprecedented levels. By 1987, it was a near-record 25.8 years for men. For women, the median age reached a record high of 23.6 years.[13] The reasons for postponing marriage vary but include such variables as economic circumstances, lifestyle choice, and a general cynicism about marriage and lifelong commitment.

Another indicator of the "marriage is optional" mentality is the increase in the number of never-marrieds. In less than two decades, the number of young adults in the twenty-something years rose by approximately 25 percent among both men and women.[14] During that same period, the number of never-married young adults in the thirty-something years also increased. That "increase among never-married people in their 30s suggests that a growing number may reject marriage entirely."[15]

Those who postpone marriage often end up postponing it permanently. An increasing proportion of middle-aged people in our society are not currently married and may never marry. The single life that used to be merely a life stage of those who were twenty-something now seems destined to become a lifelong institution for some. Singleness is no longer a transition but a lifestyle. As young singles each year swell the ranks of those who have postponed marriage indefinitely, there is a steady growth in the percentage of adults living alone. Not only is the family of the 1990s different from the family of the 1950s, but the "family" today may actually be a "non-family" composed merely of an adult living alone.

It is important to clarify that although such singles are listed by the Census Bureau as adults living alone, many are often in

Marrying Later

Median Age at First Marriage

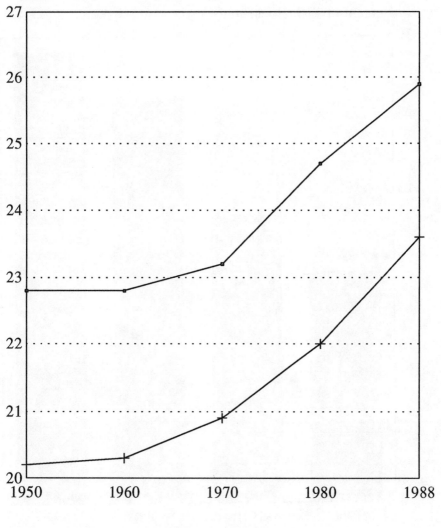

—□— Men + Women

Source: U.S. Bureau of Census.

Adults Living Alone
Non-family Households

Percent of U.S. Households

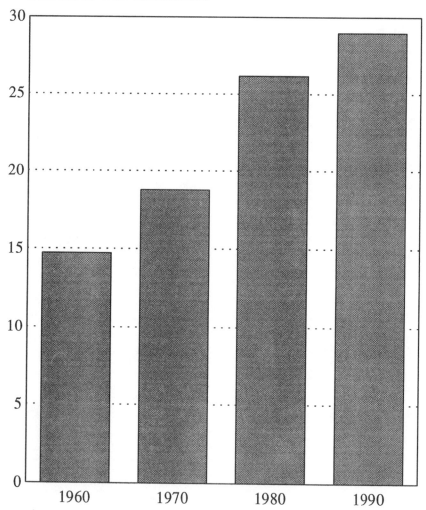

Source: U.S. Census Bureau.

some sort of tenuous relationship. The number of unmarried, co-habiting couples who are "living together" is difficult to estimate. Those transitory connections are usually relationships of convenience and have become increasingly common. It appears that at least 2.6 million households are unmarried couples, one-third of which are caring for children.

Yet even these large numbers vastly underestimate the number of people who have been cohabiting. Demographers for the National Survey of Families and Households report that among people aged twenty-five to twenty-nine, about two in ten are currently cohabiting, two in five had cohabited before their first marriage, and half of those still single had cohabited at some point.[16]

The data from this survey also show the impact of cohabitation. First, young people are entering into joint housekeeping arrangements with a partner of the opposite sex at roughly the same ages as they did in the early 1970s. "The difference is that they are using cohabitation to delay or forego marriage." Second, young people are not only postponing future marriage, they are also increasing their chances of marital failure in the future. "Contrary to popular opinion, people who cohabit before they marry are more likely to divorce. Bumpass and Sweet found that 53 percent of first marriages that start with cohabitation fail within ten years, compared with 28 percent of those where the partners did not live together."[17]

Another impact of cohabitation has been an increase in out-of-wedlock births. Cohabiting couples not only question the link between love and marriage; they also question the link between marriage and parenthood. Since the 1960s, the number of children born outside marriage has been steadily increasing. That increase includes not only the stereotypical teenage mother but a growing number of women in their twenties and thirties. Thirty percent of out-of-wedlock births in 1985 were to women aged twenty-five and older.[18]

Finally, these statistics on cohabitation should also be considered when discussing divorce. When the divorce rate began to level off and even slightly decline a decade ago, those concerned about the state of the American family began to cheer. But soon the cheers turned to groans as it became obvious that the leveling of the divorce rate was due to an increase in cohabitation. In essence, the divorce rate was down because the marriage rate was

Living Together
Unmarried Couples

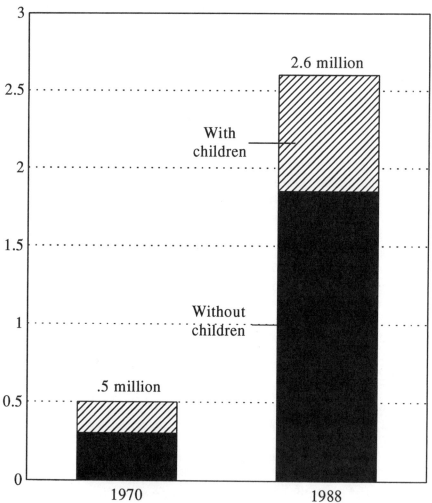

Millions of Couple Households

2.6 million

With children

Without children

.5 million

1970

1988

Source: U.S. Census Bureau.

down. Couples who break up before they marry don't show up as divorce statistics.

What the cohabitation statistics do show is how troubled relationships are for this generation. Divorce statistics substantially underrepresent the true number of relationships that come to a grinding and painful halt. Compared to earlier generations, this generation's love relationships are more turbulent and transitory. A generation searching for the storybook conclusion of living "happily ever after" frequently finds such an ending illusory. Nowhere is that more easily demonstrated than in the divorce statistics of the last few decades.

THE CHANGING DIVORCE RATE

There have always been divorces in this country. But what used to be rare and even scandalous[19] has become routine. The changing attitudes toward marriage and divorce are reflected in the changing divorce rate in this country. The graph of the U.S. divorce rate shows two significant trends. One is a sharp increase in divorces, beginning in the late 1960s and continuing through the 1970s. The second is a leveling and even slight decline in the number of divorces in the 1980s. Although the reasons behind these two phenomena are different, both are related to the attitudes of the baby boom generation toward marriage and divorce.

The increasing divorce rate in the 1970s came as baby boomers married and began families. The reasons for the increase are many and have been discussed previously: changing social attitudes toward marriage, lack of commitment to marriage, and so on.

Reasons for the more recent decrease in the divorce rate are even more complex. The divorce rate peaked in 1981 and has been headed downward ever since. Part of the reason is statistical. As the boom generation ages, it is entering the years that have traditionally had lower rates of divorce. Also, as we previously noted, fewer couples are untying the knot because *fewer couples are tying the knot*. But that is only part of the reason.

The decrease in matrimonial splits also signals a possible change in attitudes toward divorce. Couples seem determined to work harder to make their marriages work. "We went through a period when people endured their marriages; then we became a throwaway society. Now there's a new sense of hope," said Maurlea Babb, president of the Illinois Association of Marriage and Family Therapy.[20]

Births Outside Marriage

Percent Born to Unmarried Parents

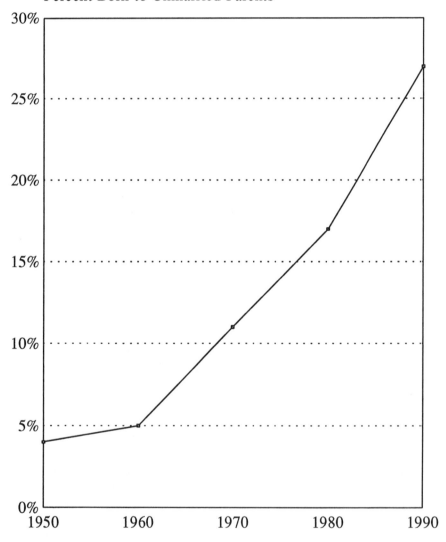

Source: U.S. Census Bureau.

The publication of books documenting the trauma of divorce have given some couples pause before they march off to the divorce courts. Psychologist Diane Medved, author of *The Case Against Divorce*, says that couples are deciding that divorce "is far more dangerous and disruptive" to their lives than staying together.[21]

Social scientists had never assumed that divorce was painless but had generally accepted the idea that it was a best alternative to troubled relationships. Diane Medved had also assumed that to be the case. But in researching her book, she came to the opposite conclusion and begins it with this startling statement:

> I have to start with a confession: This isn't the book I set out to write. I planned to write something consistent with my previous professional experience—helping people with decision making. . . . For example, I started this project believing that people who suffer over an extended period in unhappy marriages ought to get out. . . . I thought that striking down taboos about divorce was another part of the ongoing enlightenment of the women's, civil-rights, and human potential movements of the last twenty-five years. . . . To my utter befuddlement, the extensive research I conducted for this book brought me to one inescapable and irrefutable conclusion: I had been wrong.[22]

Although such conclusions do have some impact on those considering divorce, the prevailing attitude is still that divorce is preferable in many situations. A 1989 Gallup poll for *Newsweek* asked: "When husbands and wives with young children are not getting along, should they stay together for the sake of the children? Or should they separate rather than raise the children in a hostile atmosphere?" Seventy percent of the sample said "separate," whereas less than a quarter said "stay together."[23]

Other social factors also contribute to the declining divorce rate. Changing sexual mores brought on by a fear of contracting AIDS or other sexually transmitted diseases have changed sexual behavior and limited promiscuity.

Economic factors also appear to affect divorce rates. According to *Wall Street Journal* reporter Carlee Scott, a healthy economy and divorce go together.[24] When the economy worsens, couples reconsider the economic costs that result from divorce. A husband will reconsider because he might not have the financial resources to provide support, and a wife might be less willing to risk trying to support herself in an uncertain economy.

Changing Divorce Rate

Divorces per 1,000 Couples

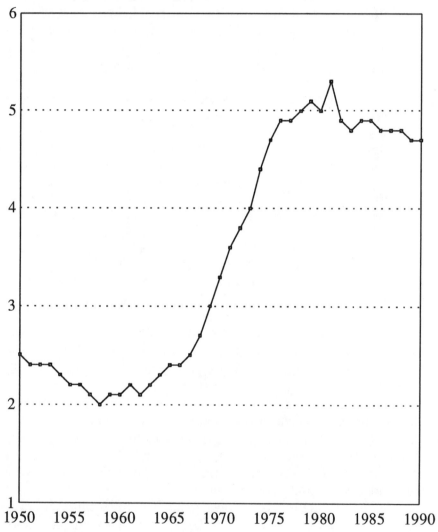

Source: National Center for Health Statistics.

MOST MARRIAGES DON'T END IN DIVORCE

Whereas there has been much concern and hand wringing over the rising divorce rate, we should not lose sight of the fact that a majority of marriages do not end in divorce court. Substantial media attention on divorce overlooks the fact that approximately fifty million established marriages are "flowing along like Ol' Man River."[25] Those marriages may run into white water and the ride may be bumpy at times, but they continue to flow along the channel of marital stability and fidelity.

Some surveys even argue that concern about rising marital infidelity is exaggerated. To listen to Alfred Kinsey or Shere Hite, one would think that steamy, daytime soap operas accurately portray the sexual behavior of typical suburban couples. But a 1990 survey by the Gallup organization provides powerful evidence to the contrary. The findings, which appear in Andrew Greeley's *Faithful Attraction*, concluded that married Americans are more monogamous than most people believed, and that fidelity and love are an integral part of most marriages.[26] Not surprisingly, the study has been criticized by researchers who have come to different conclusions. But if true, that survey paints a very different view of the American family. It found, for example, that 92 percent of married couples have not had an affair since marrying and 83 percent would marry the same person again if given the chance.[27]

THE IMPACT OF DIVORCE

For marriages that end in divorce, the impact is even greater than previously imagined. Movies such as *Kramer Versus Kramer* accurately portray the devastation of divorce on parents and children. The black comedy *The War of the Roses* depicts the hand-to-hand combat and trench warfare that occurs when two materialistic people greedily divide their property and end up demolishing their house and destroying their lives. Reality, unfortunately, is nearly as bleak and painful.

The economic impact of divorce on women can be devastating, especially if they are single mothers. Although there has been a continuing debate about the economic consequences on women, the poverty figures illustrate the point. In 1988, nearly half of single mothers were living below the poverty level,[28] compared to only 7 percent of married couples with children. By contrast, single fathers fare much better; the poverty rate is less than two in ten.[29]

Harvard sociologist Lenore Weitzman did a twenty-year study of the effects of no-fault divorce on families. Her book *The Divorce Revolution: The Unexpected Social and Economic Consequences for Women and Children in America* further documents the economic devastation on all women. Her research shows that a woman's standard of living will decline 73 percent upon divorce, whereas men experience a 42 percent increase.[30] Although later studies indicate that that statistic may be inflated,[31] low child support payments coupled with an alarmingly high rate of noncompliance by husbands nevertheless place a significant number of divorced women and their children in poverty.

In addition to the economic consequences is the educational impact. Children growing up in broken homes do not do as well in school as children from stable families. A national longitudinal survey done in 1984 found that each year spent in a single-parent family reduces a preschooler's educational attainment by one-fourth of a year. The overall average was one lost year of education for children in single-parent families.[32]

An analysis of a national survey of 17,000 children of divorce, ranging in age from infancy through seventeen years, showed the following:

- Children living with a mother and stepfather or with a divorced mother have a 20–30 percent greater risk of having had an accident or injury.
- Children living in mother-headed families were more than 50 percent more likely to have asthma.
- Children living in mother-headed families, or with mothers and stepfathers, were 40–75 percent more likely to have repeated a grade.
- Children from disrupted marriages were more than 70 percent more likely to have been suspended or expelled.[33]

But even more significant is the psychological effect of divorce, especially on children. Parents are often consoled by the notion that children will recover from the trauma of divorce. After all, if it was good for Mom or Dad, why shouldn't it also be good for the child?

Single Parents
Increase in Single-Parent Families

Percent of Family Groups with Children

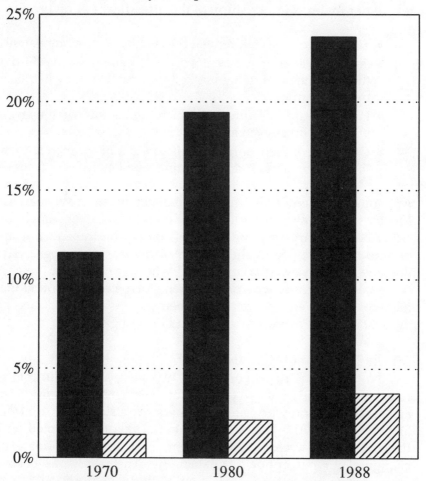

Single-mothers Single-fathers

Source: U.S. Census Bureau.

Research by psychologist Judith Wallerstein documents that some lasting wounds from divorce do not substantially diminish in time. She says, "Almost half of children of divorce enter adulthood as worried, underachieving, self-deprecating and sometimes angry young men and women."[34] In *Second Chances: Men, Women and Children a Decade After Divorce*, Wallerstein vividly illustrates the long-term psychological devastation wrought not only on the children but on the adults as well.[35] Here are just a few of her findings in her study of the aftershocks of divorce:

- Three out of five children felt rejected by at least one parent.
- Five years after their parent's divorce, more than one-third of the children were doing markedly worse than they had been before the divorce.
- Half grew up in settings in which the parents were warring with each other even after the divorce.
- One-third of the women and one-quarter of the men felt that life had been unfair, disappointing, and lonely.

Apparently the emotional tremors register on the psychological Richter scale many years after the divorce.

And, contrary to popular belief, older children do not appear to be exempt from the trauma of divorce. Sociologist Sara Bonkowski interviewed young adults who were between the ages of eighteen and thirty when their parents divorced. She found that many of them were "shattered by their parents' divorce," and almost 40 percent "expressed a deep and lingering sadness."[36]

DIVORCE, REMARRIAGE, AND STEPFAMILIES

Not only has the divorce rate increased; so has the rate of remarriage. Nearly half (46 percent) of marriages in 1990 involved at least one person who had been down the aisle before, up from 31 percent in 1970.[37] The rising number of divorces coupled with the concurrent increase in the number of remarriages seems to be changing our perception of matrimony. The result has been a pervasive and unsettling experiment with the institution.

Many remarriages are not just second marriages but third or even fourth marriages. In fact, one of the most significant predictors of divorce is a previous divorce. Remarriages experience a 60 percent divorce rate. The serial nature of divorce and remarriage has led sociologist Frank Furstenberg to identify this social pattern as "conjugal succession."[38]

More than 70 percent of divorced men and women do find new partners and eventually remarry. Thus, only about four out of ten adult Americans are currently married to their first spouse.[39] The rest are single, cohabiting, or remarried.

Because of this social shift in divorce and remarriage, demographers have begun to talk of neo-nuclear families. "Neo-nukes" are "married couples (with one or more children) in which the multiplicities of parent/child relationships are not strictly biological."[40] Such nontraditional family arrangements create a complex array of relationships linking children to parents within a single household and appear to be the wave of the future. The Stepfamily Association of America states that stepfamilies are the fastest growing family type in the U.S. It estimates that by the turn of the century stepfamilies (including those with adult children) will be the most common kind of American family.[41]

Approximately 40 percent of remarriages involve stepchildren.[42] The increasingly complex marital unions of stepfamilies are not as idyllic as portrayed in such TV sitcoms as "The Brady Bunch." Evidence is increasing that the family dynamics in remarriages differ from those in first marriages. Even those traits that might have made a first marriage successful may not work the second time around. Psychologist James Bray estimates that newly married couples face three to ten times the stress that first marriages do. The reasons include financial problems, relocation, and the tensions of dealing with stepchildren and former spouses.[43]

The stress on remarried couples is difficult enough, but it intensifies when stepchildren are involved. Conflict between a stepparent and stepchild is inevitable and can be enough to threaten the stability of the new marriage. "A 1985 study of 2,000 married and remarried people found that while 17 percent of couples with stepchildren divorced during the three year period, only 10 percent of remarried couples without stepchildren did so."[44]

Discipline is one problem. One psychological study found that "the more active a disciplinary role the stepparent played, the greater the chance that the child could experience behavioral problems during the first 2½ years of marriage."[45] Although there is some debate about whether such problems persist, many believe that they do. Psychologist Nicholas Zill found that stepchildren were "three to five times more likely to have received psychological counseling and up to twice as likely to have failed in school."[46]

Gender roles and sexuality are also an issue. Daughters who had taken on adult roles in managing the household may view a new partner as an intruder. Older children may be uncomfortable with their parents' sexuality as they are coming to grips with their own sexuality. Psychiatrist Clifford Sager warns that remarried couples need to be sexually discreet because an erotic atmosphere in a remarriage can lead to a "loosening of sexual boundaries." Such appears to be the case. Whereas only 8 percent of all children live with a stepfather, 30 percent of all cases of adult-child sexual abuse involve a stepfather.[47]

SANDWICH GENERATION

Whereas divorce has remarkably changed family relationships in the 1990s, some of the most wrenching changes have come from the coincidental nexus of two demographic trends: prolonged life span and delayed marriage. As the graying of America continues, chronic, disabling conditions will become more common. And baby boomers who delayed marriage and childbearing now find themselves "sandwiched" between child care and elder care.

The growth of the so-called sandwich generation parallels the marriage patterns previously discussed. In the past, couples typically began having children in their twenties. When their parents became frail (when they reached, say, their seventies), the children were already into their twenties and more or less independent. Now a baby boomer in his or her forties may have to care for children in grade school and high school, as well as care for parents in their seventies and eighties.

Advances in medicine have made this problem more acute. Life expectancy has increased. Men and women will spend about twice as many adult years with a surviving parent than they would have in 1900.[48] And whereas modern medicine has been able to increase the quantity of life, often it has not been as successful at improving the quality of life. More than six million elderly Americans need help with such basic tasks as getting out of bed and going to the bathroom, and countless other millions cannot manage meals, money, or transportation.[49]

The circumstances of the sandwich generation are varied. Young couples already frustrated in attempts to find quality day care for their children now must diligently search for a good elderly care program for their parents. Middle-aged couples find themselves overwhelmed by the simultaneous economic demands for their kids' college tuition and their parents' healthcare. Spouses, in their golden years, spend most of their time taking care of an ailing mate. Each circumstance is different, but the financial and emotional pressure on families is the same.

The latest twist has been the "boomerang kids." Children in their twenties, like the swallows of Capistrano, are returning to the nest in record numbers. Reversing the trend of the baby boom generation, members of the current generation of kids are moving back in with their parents until they can establish themselves on a firmer economic foundation.

In the 1960s and 1970s, baby boomers couldn't wait to get out of the house. At the turn of the century, the average man departed his parents' house at the age of twenty-three. By the 1970s, the average male was leaving home at nineteen.[50] But changing social and economic conditions in the 1990s have forced many fledglings back to the nest.

Whatever the circumstances, national surveys confirm that the primary burden of the sandwich generation falls upon women,[51] causing many to refer to it as "the daughter track." In the 1980s, when some wanted to separate women into "career primary" and "career and family oriented" tracks, some dubbed the latter the "mommy track." Just when women on the "mommy track" thought they could get back to their careers, many are finding themselves switched to an even longer "daughter track." A 1988 House of Representatives report estimates that the average American woman will spend seventeen years rearing children and eighteen years helping aging parents.[52]

Until recently, women were in the home and thus were the primary caregivers for both young and old. Now more than half of women who care for elderly parents and relatives also work outside the home, and 40 percent of those women are still rearing their own children.[53] Nevertheless, they are still caught in the expectations of a previous age and are forced to balance time, money, and family priorities in the midst of conflicting needs and demands.

Wives who are looking for help may be disappointed. Husbands may be unable, or perhaps unwilling, to confront the physical and emotional needs of aging parents, especially if they are expected to shoulder the additional financial burdens engendered by the sandwich generation. Enlisting the help of brothers and sisters may also be difficult and may resurface simmering sibling rivalries. Boomers in midlife, struggling with the future prospects of their own mortality and mindful of some of their pain in childhood, may consciously or unconsciously turn their backs on their frail parents and other members of the family. Women on the "daughter track" often are left to pick up the pieces.

Caregivers quickly find that time becomes a precious commodity and face a crisis of priorities when too many choices meet too little time. Finding time and keeping sanity can often seem difficult whether rearing children or caring for elderly parents. Doing both simultaneously may be more than many family relationships can stand. As one caregiver aptly put it, "Look at the metaphor. Sandwich generation. What's in the middle? Chopped meat."[54]

Caregivers are often unprepared for the circumstances of the sandwich generation. Responsibilities can come suddenly. A stroke, a heart attack, or a broken hip can quickly change established lifestyles and confront members of the sandwich generation with decisions for which they are unprepared. Role reversal also catches this generation off-guard. One day you are your parents' child. The next day you effectively become the parent, and your parents are in the child role. Parenting your parents can surface an array of questions and emotions.

The impact is not only emotional; it is economic. Families with little discretionary income are caught in a triple squeeze of trying to provide for their children's education, their parents' healthcare needs, and their own retirement. As we will discuss in a subsequent chapter, that is another reason this generation faces a crisis of financial security.

The financial crisis intensifies for many families when the primary caregiver (usually the wife) must cut back or leave work in order to cope with the demands at home. According to the American Association of Retired Persons, about 14 percent of caregivers have switched from full-time to part-time jobs, and 12 percent have left the work force altogether.[55] Many more have considered quitting their jobs and may do so in the coming years.

A CRISIS OF LONELINESS: IN FAMILY AND COMMUNITY

As families turn inward and struggle to make ends meet, and as others find themselves alone due to divorce or lifestyle choice, loneliness looms on the horizon. Not only is loneliness found within families; it's found within communities. In the early

1830s, Alexis de Tocqueville wrote in *Democracy in America* that "democracy does not create strong attachments." American society has always produced "Lone Rangers." But the current economic and social trends have further accentuated that individualism and isolation.

Also contributing to the social isolation is the loss of a middle-class values consensus. As the middle class shrinks and the pace of life increases, the sense of community disappears. "Neighbors no longer share common aspirations or values. Struggling just to maintain their standard of living, people don't have time for their families, let alone their neighbors."[56]

The town square has been replaced by enclosed shopping malls as a popular meeting place. But instead of being a place where people linger and talk, the more than 25,000 malls in this country are merely a place for busy people to converge and say hi or quickly shop as they rush off to other pressing activities.

Deep and enduring relationships within the family and within community are now the exception. Most have few, if any, relationships they can count on in times of need. As this generation becomes more isolated from family and community, a crisis of loneliness seems inevitable.

NOTES

1. "When the 'Family' Will Have a New Definition," What the Next 50 Years Will Bring, a special edition of *U.S. News and World Report,* 9 May 1983, A-3.
2. Robert Bellah et al. *Habits of the Heart* (Berkeley, Calif.: Univ. of California, 1985), 108.
3. Landon Jones, *Great Expectations: America and the Baby Boom Generation* (New York: Ballantine, 1980), 307.
4. Martha Farnsworth Riche, "The Postmarital Society," *American Demographics,* November 1988, 23.
5. *The Public Pulse,* May 1989.
6. *MassMutual American Values Study,* July 1989.
7. *What's Happening to American Families,* October 1988, 22.
8. *MassMutual Study,* 29–30.
9. "The 21st Century Family," *Newsweek Special Edition,* Winter/Spring 1990, 18.
10. *What's Happening to American Families,* October 1988, 12.
11. Riche, "The Postmarital Society," 23, 25.
12. Ibid., 23.
13. Ibid., 24.
14. Ibid.

15. Ibid.

16. Ibid., 25–26.

17. Ibid., 26.

18. Ibid.

19. The discussion of Nelson Rockefeller's presidential bid well illustrates the changing perception of divorce. Many wondered whether he could be elected president in 1964 simply because he had been divorced. A decade later, divorce was not even an issue discussed in the candidacies of Gerald Ford and Ronald Reagan.

20. Quoted in Carlee Scott, "As Baby Boomers Age, Fewer Couples Untie the Knot," *Wall Street Journal*, 7 November 1990, B-1.

21. Ibid.

22. Diane Medved, *The Case Against Divorce* (New York: Donald I. Fine, 1989), 1-2.

23. "The 21st Century Family," 18.

24. Scott, "As Baby Boomers Age," B-1.

25. Pollster Louis Harris first used this phrase in the 1980s to illustrate his concern regarding the misuse of the statistic that one out of every two marriages end in divorce.

26. "Marital Fidelity Thriving, Poll Finds," *Dallas Morning News*, 12 February 1990, 3A.

27. Nanci Hellmich, "Fidelity of Marriage," *USA Today*, 12 February 1990, A-1.

28. Some single parents began as single by having children out of wedlock. But the growing number of single women who are the head of households is due in large part to divorce.

29. Saul D. Hoffman and Greg J. Duncan, *American Demographics*, March 1989, 13.

30. Lenore J. Weitzman, "Splitting Up," *USA Today*, 27 February 1990, 9A.

31. Saul Hoffman and Greg Duncan argue in the November 1988 issue of *Demography* that the findings by Lenore Weitzman "are almost certainly in error." They agree that a woman's income declines but not as dramatically. Martha Farnsworth Riche, "The Wrong Number," *American Demographics*, March 1989, 13.

32. Sheila Fitzgerald Klein and Andrea Beller, *American Demographics*, March 1989, 13.

33. Alan Otten, "Baby Boomer People: Make Less, But Make Do," *Wall Street Journal*, 5 July 1990.

34. Anastasia Toufexis, "The Lasting Wounds of Divorce," *Time*, 6 February 1989, 61.

35. Judith Wallerstein and Sandra Blakeslee, *Second Chances: Men, Women and Children A Decade After Divorce* (New York: Ticknor & Fields, 1989).

36. Sara Bonkowski, "Lingering Sadness: Young Adults' Response to Parental Divorce," *Social Casework*, April 1989, 219–23.

37. William Dunn, "I Do, Is Repeat Refrain for Half of Newlyweds," *USA Today*, 15 February 1991, A-1.

38. Art Levine, "The Second Time Around: Realities of Remarriage," *U.S. News and World Report*, 29 January 1990, 50.

39. Ibid.

40. "Families: Neo-Nukes," *Research Alert*, 17 August 1990, 6.

41. Eric Miller et al., *Future Vision: The 189 Most Important Trends of the 1990s* (Naperville, Ill.: Sourcebooks Trade, 1991), 42.

42. Levine, "The Second Time Around," 51.

43. Quoted in ibid., 50.

44. Ibid., 51.

45. Ibid.

46. Quoted in ibid.

47. Ibid.

48. Barbara Vobejda, "Sandwich Generation Cares for Elderly," *Houston Chronicle*, 26 February 1991, 3.

49. Melinda Beck, "Trading Places," *Newsweek*, 16 July 1990, 48.

50. Jones, *Great Expectations*, 204.

51. Ethel Sharp, "Seniority: Comfort and Care," *St. Petersburg Times*, 26 March 1991, 20X.

52. Beck, "Trading Places," *Newsweek*, 49.

53. Ibid., 48-49.

54. Vobejda, "Sandwich Generation," *Houston Chronicle*, 3.

55. Beck, "Trading Places," 49.

56. John Koten, "The Shattered Middle Class," *Wall Street Journal*, 11 March 1987.

CHAPTER EIGHT
THE CRISIS OF LONELINESS

Turning thirty was traumatic for Teri. It wasn't the birthday itself that affected her as much as the loneliness. In high school and college, Teri was surrounded by lots of friends. But her network of friends began to unravel when she headed out into the work force. She was unprepared for the loneliness of the single career woman.

Like most women, she expected to find the man of her dreams and get married. Though she occasionally dated, Teri never got serious with anyone. She was busy with her career and began to find that, as she pursued that, the number of eligible men in her life soon dwindled.

Even more disconcerting was the loss of female friends. As each of the women in her life got married, she moved out of Teri's life. By her late twenties, Teri began to notice that many of the single women she counted as acquaintances became more distant. Perhaps they perceived her beauty as a threat to their ability to attract a man. Perhaps it was envy of her career success. Perhaps it was the busyness of Teri's life. Whatever the reason, Teri found herself isolated and alone.

When Shelley—one of Teri's college roommates—came into town, she was surprised to find Shelley equally isolated. Married since college, Shelley confided over lunch one day that she felt as lonely as Teri. While Shelley's husband, Bob, was busy with his career, Shelley stayed at home with the kids. They had moved two times in the last five years, so Shelley had few friends in her neighborhood. Though she was not alone literally, Shelley felt just as lonely as Teri. Even though Teri and Shelley had different social circumstances, they shared at least one thing in common: they were very much alone.

Teri and Shelley are not unique. The baby boom generation is headed for a crisis of loneliness. The reasons are demographics and social isolation. More boomers are living alone than in previous generations, and those living with another person still feel nagging pangs of loneliness.

In previous centuries where extended families dominated the social landscape, the concept of a sizable proportion of adults living alone was unthinkable. Even in this century, adults living alone have usually been found near the beginning (singles) and end (widows) of adult life. But that period is now longer because of lifestyle choices on the front end and advances in modern medicine on the back end. Baby boomers are postponing marriage and thus extending the number of years of being single. Moreover, their parents are (and presumably they will be) living longer, thereby increasing the number of years one adult will be living by himself or herself.

Yet the increase in the number of adults living alone can be attributed to more than just changes at the beginning and end of adult life. Increasing numbers of boomers are living most or all of their adult life alone.

In the 1950s, about one in every ten households had only one person in them. Those were primarily widows. But today, due to the three D's of social statistics (death, divorce, and deferred marriage), about one in every four households is a single-person household.[1] If current trends continue, sociologists predict that that ratio will increase to one in every three households by the twenty-first century.

In the past, gender differences were a significant factor in determining the number of adults living alone. For example, young single households are more likely to be men, since women marry younger. On the other hand, old single households are more likely to be women, because women live longer than men.[2]

Although those trends still hold true in general, the gender distinctions are blurring as boomers of both sexes reject traditional attitudes toward marriage. As we mentioned in the previous chapter and will develop further here, boomers differ from their parents in three significant marriage patterns: they are marrying less, marrying later, and staying married for shorter periods of time.

The most marriageable generation in history has not made the trip to the altar in the same percentage as its parents. In 1946, the parents of the baby boom set an all-time record of 2,291,000 marriages. That record was not broken during the late 1960s and early 1970s, when millions of boomers entered the marriage-prone years. Finally, in 1979 the record that had lasted thirty-three years was broken when the children of the baby boom made 2,317,000 marriages.[3] Singleness has become a lifestyle for a record number of baby boomers. Whereas their parents saw marriage as a necessity, boomers see marriage as an option.

Instead of marrying, many boomers chose to "live together." When this generation entered the traditional years of marriage-ability, the number of unmarried couples living together in the United States doubled in just ten years to well over a million. The sharpest change was among cohabiting couples under twenty-five, who increased ninefold after 1970.[4] Demographers estimate that as many as 1.5 to 2 million couples have cohabited in the U.S.[5] Yet even those high figures underestimate the lifestyle changes of boomers. The numbers merely represent the number of couples living together *at any one time*. Cohabitation is a fluid state, so the total number living together or living alone is in the several millions.

Second, boomers are not only marrying less; they are marrying later. Until the baby boom generation arrived on the scene, the median age of marriage remained stable. But since the mid-fifties, the median age of first marriage has been edging up. Now both "men and women are marrying a full eighteen months later than their counterparts a generation earlier."[6]

That trend has also extended the single years much longer than any previous generation. As careers, economic circumstances, and lifestyle choices postpone marriage, unmarried men and women have learned to adapt and have created a singles lifestyle. A society of lonely, single people has spawned a culture to meet their needs for companionship. There are singles clubs, dating services, dance clubs, hiking clubs, and dining clubs. Adult

Increase in Singles
Childless Single Person Households

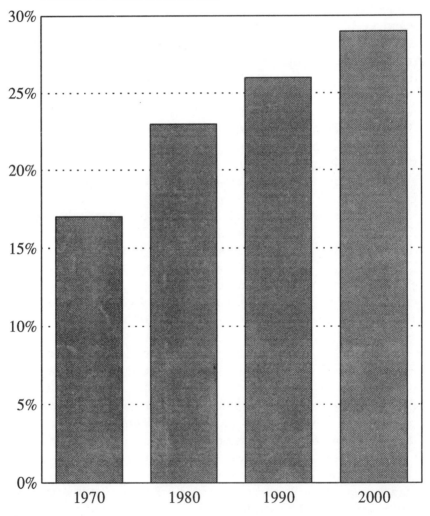

Percent of total households

Source: Harvard Joint Center for Housing Studies.

education programs provide additional points of contact through such courses as "culinary courtship" and "100 romantic things to do around the metroplex." And for affluent singles, there are ski vacations, cruise ships, and Club Med programs.

Although many of the elements of the singles lifestyle were designed to cope with singleness, they have, in many cases, served to extend singleness and postpone marriage. Here again is another difference between baby boomers and their parents. Whereas their parents saw singleness as something to avoid, many baby boomers see it as something to prolong.

Finally, boomers do not stay married as long as their parents. As we have already noted, boomers have the highest divorce rate of any generation in history. But that is only part of the statistical picture. They also divorce earlier. When the divorce rate shot up in the sixties and seventies, the increase did not come from empty nesters finally filing for divorce after sending their children into the world. Instead, it came from young couples divorcing before they even had children. Demographer Tobert Michael of Stanford calculated that whereas men and women in their twenties comprised only about 20 percent of the population, they contributed 60 percent of the growth in the divorce rate in the sixties and early seventies.[7]

Taken together, such statistics point to a coming crisis of loneliness for the boom generation. More and more middle-aged adults will find themselves living alone. Thomas Exter, writing in *American Demographics*, predicted that "The most dramatic growth in single-person households should occur among those aged 45 to 64, as baby boomers become middle-aged." Those households are expected to increase by 42 percent, and it appears that the number of men living alone is growing faster than the number of women.[8]

LIVING–TOGETHER LONELINESS

The crisis of loneliness will affect more than the increasing number of baby boomers living alone. Although that increase is staggering and unprecedented, the numbers are fractional compared with the number of baby boomers in relationships that leave them feeling very much alone.

The "c" word (as it was often called in the eighties) is a significant issue. Commitment is a foreign concept to most of the million-plus cohabiting couples. Such fluid and highly mobile situations often form out of convenience and demonstrate little of the commitment necessary to make a relationship work. The relationships are transitory and form and dissolve with alarming frequency. Anyone looking for intimacy and commitment will not find them in this kind of relationship.

Commitment is also a problem in marriages. Spawned in the streams of sexual freedom and multiple lifestyle options, boomers may be less committed to making marriage work than previous generations. Marriages that are supposed to be the source of stability and intimacy often produce uncertainty and isolation. Spouses end up feeling pangs of loneliness.

In many cases, loneliness has less to do with the relationship itself than with the person in the relationship. Psychologist and bestselling author Dan Kiley has coined the term "living-together loneliness," or LTL, to describe that phenomenon.[9] He has estimated that ten to twenty million people (primarily women) suffer from LTL.

LTL is an affliction of the individual, not the relationship, though that may be troubled too. Kiley believes LTL has more to do with two issues previously discussed: the changing roles of men and women and the crisis of expectations. In the last few decades, especially following the rise of the modern feminist movement, expectations that men have of women and women have of men have been significantly altered. When such expectations do not match reality, disappointment (and eventually loneliness) sets in.

Kiley first noted this phenomenon among his female patients in 1970. He began to realize that loneliness comes in two varieties. The first is the loneliness felt by single, shy people who have no friends. The second is more elusive because it involves the person in a relationship who nevertheless feels isolated and alone. According to Kiley, "There is nothing in any diagnostic or statistical manual about this. I found out about it by listening to people."[10] He has discovered that some men have similar feelings, but most LTL sufferers tend to be women. The typical LTL sufferer is a woman between the ages of thirty-three and forty-six, married, and living a comfortable life. She may also have children. She blames her husband or live-in partner for her loneliness, and he's often critical, demanding, and uncommunicative.

The typical LTL woman realizes she is becoming obsessed with her bitterness and is often in counseling for depression or anxiety. She is frequently isolated and feels some estrangement from other people, even close friends. Sometimes she will have a fantasy about her partner dying, believing that her loneliness will end if that man is out of her life.

To determine if a woman is a victim of LTL, Kiley employs a variation of an "uncoupled loneliness" scale devised by researchers at the University of California at Los Angeles.[11] For example, an LTL woman would agree with the following propositions:

- I can't turn to him when I feel bad.
- I feel left out of his life.
- I feel isolated from him, even when he's in the same room.
- I am unhappy being shut off from him.
- No one really knows me well.

Kiley also documents five identifiable stages of LTL that are likely to affect baby boom women. A typical LTL woman who marries at about age twenty-two will feel bewildered until she is twenty-eight. At that point isolation sets in. At thirty-four, she begins to feel agitated. That turns to depression between the ages of forty-three and fifty. After that, the woman faces absolute exhaustion.

Women also face loneliness as homemakers left at home to rear the children. According to sociologist Tony Campolo, that is a unique by-product of modern society.

It must be noted that no woman in history has been left so alone to face the responsibilities of childrearing as has the contemporary mother. In earlier times, people lived in small communities, surrounded by kinfolk or intimate friends. These close associates often had a wealth of experience in motherhood that they shared with the new mother. They also took care of the children from time to time, providing her with needed rest and relief. If she wanted to go to town with her husband, there was always an aunt, an in-law, a sister, or a close neighbor who would come in and mind the children.[12]

A woman in today's world finds herself isolated. She may live in a high-rise apartment or a within a suburban tract, but she is surrounded by strangers. When she is sick or needs help with the children, no one is there for her. When her husband leaves for the office, her only contact with him may be an afternoon phone call. Instead of depending on family members, she must depend upon baby-sitters and day-care facilities.

Women of the baby boom find that loneliness has become a part of their lives, whether they are living alone or rearing a family. But women are not the only ones to face a crisis of loneliness; baby boom men will face a crisis that is as great, if not greater.

MALE LONELINESS

Many studies have concluded that women have better relational skills, which help them become successful at making and keeping friends than men. For example, women are more likely than men to express their emotions and display empathy and compassion in response to the emotions of others.[13] Men, on the other hand, are frequently more isolated and competitive and therefore have fewer (if any) close friends.

Men, in fact, may not even be conscious of their loneliness and isolation. In *The Hazards of Being Male: The Myth of Masculine Privilege*, Herb Goldberg asks adult men if they have any close friends. Most of them seemed surprised by the question and usually responded, "No, why? Should I?"[14]

David Smith lists in *Men Without Friends* the following six characteristics of men that prove to be barriers to friendship.[15] First, men show an aversion to showing emotions. Expressing feelings is generally taboo for males. At a young age, boys receive the cultural message that they are to be strong and stoic, so as men they shun emotions. Such an aversion makes deep relationships difficult.

Second, men seemingly have an inherent inability to fellowship. In fact, men find it hard to accept the fact that they need fellowship. If someone suggests having lunch together, it is often met with the response, "Sure, what's up?" Men may get together for business, sports, or recreation (hunting and fishing), but they rarely do so just to enjoy each other's company. Centering a meeting on an activity is not bad, but the conversation often does not move beyond work or sports to deeper levels.

Third, men have inadequate role models. The male macho image prevents strong friendships since a mask of aggressiveness and strength keeps men from knowing themselves and others.

A fourth barrier is male competition. Men are inordinately competitive. They feel they must excel in what they do, yet that competitive spirit is frequently a barrier to friendship.

Fifth, men frequently seem unable to ask for help because they perceive it as a sign of weakness or don't want to burden their family or colleagues with their problems. In the end, male attempts at self-sufficiency rob them of fulfilling relationships.

A final barrier Smith states is incorrect priorities. Men often have a distorted order of priorities where physical things are more important than relationships. Success and status are determined by material wealth rather than by the number of close friends one has.

Any or all of those characteristics pose barriers for male friendships. Loneliness and isolation are further intensified by the busyness of career and family. As noted in the previous chapter, baby boomers are finding less time to devote to any activity, including building relationships.

Yet another reason for male loneliness is the propensity for men to define and limit their identity. H. Norman Wright warns:

> The more a man centers his identity in just one phase of his life—such as vocation, family, or career—the more vulnerable he is to threats against his identity and the more prone he is to experience a personal crisis. A man who has limited sources of identity is potentially the most fragile. Men need to broaden their basis for identity. They need to see themselves in several roles rather than *just* a teacher, *just* a salesman, *just* a handsome, strong male, *just* a husband.[16]

Many men limit their acquaintances to just one phase of their life: usually their work. When they change jobs or face a career struggle, they are effectively cut off from their only source of encouragement and support—hence they, too, feel the nagging pains of loneliness.

OUR LONELY SOCIETY

Loneliness is not just a problem of the individual. It is endemic to our modern, urban society. In rural communities, although the farm houses are far apart, community is usually very strong. Yet in today's urban and suburban communities, people are physically close to each other but emotionally distant. Close proximity does not translate into close community.

Roberta Hestenes has referred to that concept as "crowded loneliness."

> Today we are seeing the breakdown of natural 'community' network groups in neighborhoods like relatives, PTA, etc. At

the same time, we have relationships with so many people. Twenty percent of the American population moves each year. If they think they are moving, they won't put down roots. People don't know how to reach out and touch people. This combination produces crowded loneliness.[17]

That is the most curious aspect of loneliness in modern society. Usually when we think of loneliness we mean that no one is around, that we are alone. Yet loneliness in a crowd can be much worse. We are surrounded by people, but they are not interested in us or our needs. We feel isolated and cut off. That sort of loneliness is more insidious because we are constantly reminded by the people around us that we do not belong and that nobody really cares.

German sociologist Ferdinand Tornies described two different kinds of societies. The first was *gemeinschaft*. This society was committed to community, tradition, intimacy, and kinship, and it fostered a sense of belonging. The second was *gesellschaft*. It was a group that was created for a special interest or purpose. Members freely form an association as a means of achieving some common purpose. Whatever its structure in the past, American society today resembles the latter more than the former. Americans generally and baby boomers specifically are individualists who pursue their goals and dreams as individuals rather than as a cohesive group.

Another reason for social isolation is the American desire for privacy. Though many boomers desire community and long for a greater intimacy with other members of their generation, they will choose privacy even if it means a nagging loneliness. In his book *We the Lonely People*, Ralph Keyes says that above all else Americans value mobility, privacy, and convenience.[18] Those three values make developing a sense of community almost impossible.

In *A Nation of Strangers*, Vance Packard argues that the mobility of American society contributed to social isolation and loneliness. He described five forms of uprooting that were creating greater distances between people.[19]

1. *The uprooting of people who move again and again.* An old Carole King song asks, "Doesn't anybody stay in one place any more?" When Packard wrote his book, he estimated that the average American would move about fourteen times in his or her lifetime.

By contrast, he estimated that the average Japanese would move five times.[20]

2. *The uprooting that occurs when communities undergo upheaval.* The accelerated population growth during the baby boom along with urban renewal and flight to the suburbs have been disruptive to previously stable communities.

3. *The uprooting from housing changes within communities.* The proliferation of multiple-dwelling units in urban areas crowd people together who frequently live side by side in anonymity.

4. *Increasing isolation due to work schedules.* When continuous-operation plants and offices dominate an area's economy, neighbors remain strangers.

5. *The accelerating fragmentation of the family.* The steady rise in the number of broken families and the segmentation of the older population from the younger heightens social isolation.

Other social commentators believe that the degeneration into a society of isolation and narcissism corresponds with the rise of a media culture. First was the printing press. Marshall McLuhan has argued that the print revolution began to isolate people from their community in ways not experienced by tribes and villages in preliterate times.[21] Elizabeth Eisenstein noted that "The conditions of scribal culture . . . held narcissism in check." But print allowed it to break free.[22]

Moreover, by its very nature reading is a socially isolating activity. Except for the times when one is reading to a group, reading the printed page demands an isolated reader and an engaged mind.

Neil Postman further argues that not only is reading an isolating event, so is broadcast media. Families may talk of watching television together, but that is a fiction. "Like other media, such as radio and records, television tends to be an isolating experience, requiring no conformity to rules of public behavior. It does not even require that you pay attention, and, as a consequence, does nothing to further an adult awareness of social cohesion."[23]

When taken together, the various factors show a crisis of loneliness for the baby boom generation. Everyone in this generation will no doubt feel the hollow pain of loneliness and therefore experience its consequences.

THE CONSEQUENCES OF LONELINESS

A generation of lonely people will produce social consequences. Student revolutions on campus during the 1960s were testimony to the consequences of alienated, rebellious youth. Similar, but less confrontational, changes are likely in the coming decades.

The number of people who feel alienated, disconnected, or simply cut off is likely to increase. In the fifties, Harvard sociologist George Homans warned that one of the social consequences of the fragmentation of social groups would be loneliness and a legacy of coldness.[24] Many boomers who were the lonely children of lonely parents grow up with cold personalities and were unable to make intimate contact with others.

Another social consequence of loneliness will be the nagging question, Who will care for me? Previous generations looked to their families as a source of security. But with fewer baby boomers forming families and with less stability and commitment in those that are formed, they face an impending crisis of security.

We will consider this issue more fully in the next chapter, but for now, notice the irony. Baby boomers live in a world full of insecurity. Careers are unstable; pensions are insecure. Social Security isn't secure. And with bank failures and stock market crashes, this generation needs something to depend on in the future.

In the past, the family was the bedrock of security but no longer. Boomers may well ask, "Who will care for me?" The troubling answer will either be that there is no one around to care for me, or that those who are around (spouse, children) may be unable or unwilling to do so.

The psychological consequences of loneliness are cause for concern. Back in 1959, a lead article in *Psychiatry* raised the possibility that loneliness plays an important part in mental disorders. Later, other investigators found that certain types of schizophrenia have their highest incidence among rooming-house and hotel lodgers, who tend to be very lonely people. Finally, C. Tieze and associates found support for the view that the duration of residence in a particular house is related to personality disorders. They found the disorders to be higher among people who had short periods of residence than among those who had lived in the same house at least ten years.[25] Many researchers believe that social instability and isolation are contributing factors to many personality disorders.[26]

The medical consequences of loneliness are equally troubling. Whether it be cancer or coronary heart disease, lonely people seem to be more prone to serious illness. As far back as 1971, Clause Bahnson proposed in an American Cancer Society Seminar that a high proportion of cancer patients show a tendency to be lonely, emotionally isolated, and have difficulty forming deep relationships with other people.[27]

James Lynch has documented many of the other effects of loneliness in *The Broken Heart: The Medical Consequences of Loneliness*. "Almost every segment of our society seems to be deeply afflicted by one of the major diseases of our age—human loneliness. The price we are paying for our failure to understand our biological needs for love and human companionship may be ultimately exacted in our own hearts and blood vessels."[28]

Social statistics are replete with correlations between living alone and increased mortality: increased number of male suicides, increased number of heart attacks, increased incidence of depression, to mention just a few. Dr. Lynch found that unmarried people visit physicians more often and stay in hospitals longer than married people with the same illnesses. And people who have never married are seven times more likely to be admitted to mental hospitals.[29]

More recent studies of the effect of loneliness on physical health further corroborate those earlier findings:

> One experience stressful to virtually everyone, apparently is loneliness. A large body of evidence now shows that people who feel alone in the world, uninvolved with other people and their community, run a high risk of illness, including heart disease. Heart-attack survivors are at especially high risk. In one study, people who were found through questionnaires and interviews to be socially isolated and to have a high degree of psychosocial stress—unhappiness with job or marriage, for example—were four times more likely to die from a second heart attack than those with the lowest levels of stress and isolation.[30]

Two independent studies, one done at the University of California at Berkeley and the University of Michigan, found that adults who do not belong to nurturing groups or relationships have a death rate twice as high as those with frequent caring contact. Dr.

James S. House of the University of Michigan said, "The data indicates that social isolation is as significant to mortality as smoking, high blood pressure, high cholesterol, obesity, and lack of physical exercise."[31]

Mix one part stress (from a baby boomer's frenetic lifestyle) with the one part loneliness that often accompanies a boomer's lifestyle choices, and you have a corrosive mixture that disintegrates both body and soul. A generation bent on going it alone will no doubt encounter social as well as medical problems in the coming decades.

All of that will indeed culminate in the nagging question, Who will care for me? With families less stable and the economic horizon less secure, baby boomers face an impending crisis of security. Who will take care of single adults in their later years? Do families have the financial resources to provide for themselves in the future?

NOTES

1. George Masnick and Mary Jo Bane, *The Nation's Families 1960-1990*, cited in *The Disappearance of Childhood* (New York: Dell, 1982).
2. Thomas Exter, "Alone at Home," *American Demographics*, April 1990, 55.
3. Landon Jones, *Great Expectations: America and the Baby Boom Generation* (New York: Ballantine, 1980), 208.
4. Ibid., 207.
5. Varying estimates can be found in such articles as "Love and the Law," *Mademoiselle*, September 1982, 146, and "Two Million Couples Living Together," *Dallas Times Herald*, October 20, 1977.
6. Jones, *Great Expectations*, 208.
7. Ibid., 215.
8. Exter, *American Demographics*, 55. Thomas Exter predicts that the number of men aged forty-five to sixty-four living alone will increase 50 percent and the number of women living alone will increase 35 percent. The numerical increase for each sex will be about 1.1 million additional households.
9. Dan Kiley, *Living Together, Feeling Alone: Healing Your Hidden Loneliness* (New York: Prentice-Hall, 1989).
10. Dixie Reed, "Alone Together," *Dallas Times Herald*, 20 November 1989, B-1, 3.
11. Ibid., B-3.
12. Anthony Campolo, *The Success Fantasy* (Wheaton, Ill.: Victor, 1980), 93.
13. "Men vs. Women," *U.S. News and World Report*, 8 August 1988, 54.
14. Herb Goldberg, *The Hazards of Being Male: The Myth of Masculine Privilege* (New York: New American Library, 1976).

15. David W. Smith, *Men Without Friends* (Nashville: Nelson, 1990), 24–30.
16. H. Norman Wright, *Seasons of a Marriage* (Ventura, Calif.: Regal, 1982), 75.
17. Quoted in Dennis Rainey, *Lonely Husbands, Lonely Wives* (Dallas: Word, 1989), 11–12.
18. Ralph Keyes, *We the Lonely People,* quoted in Smith, *Men Without Friends,* 169.
19. Vance Packard, *A Nation of Strangers* (New York: David McKay, 1972), 2–5.
20. Ibid., 6–7.
21. Marshall McLuhan, *Understanding Media* (New York: New American Library, 1964).
22. Elizabeth Eisenstein, *The Printing Press As an Agent of Change* (Cambridge, England: Cambridge Univ., 1979), 233.
23. Neil Postman, *The Disappearance of Childhood* (New York: Dell, 1982), 114.
24. George C. Homans, *The Human Group* (New York: Harcourt, Brace, Jovanovich, 1950), 457.
25. C. Tieze, P. Lemkau, M. Cooper, "Personality Disorder and Spatial Mobility," *American Journal of Sociology,* 1, 1942.
26. Robert A. Nisbet, *Community and Power* (London: Oxford Univ., 1962), 18.
27. "Who Gets Cancer?" *Newsweek,* 19 April 1971.
28. James Lynch, *The Broken Heart: The Medical Consequences of Loneliness* (New York: Basic Books, 1977), 8, 14.
29. Ibid.
30. Steve Findlay, "The Pressure-Cooker Factor," *U.S. News and World Report,* 6 August 1990, 62.
31. Quote by James S. House in Smith, *Men Without Friends,* 46–47.

CHAPTER NINE
THE CRISIS OF SECURITY

Bob and Jan had a dream: to take early retirement and enjoy themselves while they still had their health. Bob wanted to write the great American novel. Jan wanted to buy a recreational vehicle and see the country. They would pack their camper with clothes and a laptop computer and enjoy a life of leisure—traveling by day and typing by night.

Unfortunately, their dream seems to be fading into the mist. Though still in their late forties, Bob and Jan are becoming more aware with each passing day that their dream of early retirement will not materialize. Although there is a growing sum in Bob's pension funds, little else is available for early retirement. Most of the money they saved from Jan's job went to pay the high cost of college for their two sons. The rest went for various items: family vacations, a new car, medical bills for Jan's mother. They put thousands and thousands of dollars of their earnings into their beautiful home, which now seems wasted since they probably will have to sell their house for much less than they paid for it. The money they would need for early retirement just isn't there.

As the prospects of early retirement fade into the distance, Bob and Jan wonder if a comfortable retirement is possible at all. Even postponing their retirement dreams to age sixty-five does not seem likely to resolve the financial pressures. Many of the same economic realities that killed their dream of early retirement now seem to be conspiring to make any future plans for retirement less than promising. The retirement that once looked so bright is now looking dismal.

Bob and Jan are not alone. Like others in their generation, they are facing the harsh economic realities that will affect their financial future. Part of the reason for these financial circumstances is demographics. Preceding and succeeding the baby boom were consecutive years of fewer births. Thirty-five percent more Americans were born during the baby boom than during the previous nineteen years, and 12 percent more were born than during the subsequent nineteen years.[1] That nineteen-year blip in fertility has created more than just an oddity in social statistics. It has clouded the future of baby boomers.

The elderly are supported, especially during the waning years of their old age, by members of the younger generation. The baby boom was immediately followed by a baby bust, or what many commentators have labeled a birth dearth. The disproportionate ratio between baby boomers and baby busters raises questions about the boom generation's future and suggests they will face an impending crisis of security.

BOOMERS' FINANCIAL FUTURE

Though optimistic in its youth, the boom generation has grown increasingly pessimistic in the 1990s, especially about their financial future. As one commentator put it, "Americans overwhelmingly view the 1990s as a decade of fewer economic opportunities and mounting financial burdens."[2]

Their concern arises from both economic and demographic realities. The harsh economic reality in the 1990s is the federal deficit, which mushroomed during the 1980s and created many other economic problems. In the first half of the 1980s, the national debt increased by more than twice the amount incurred during the previous two centuries.[3] By the mid-1980s interest on the national debt approached $180 billion. That was nearly 19 percent of all federal spending. Put another way, the amount nearly equaled the total spent on Social Security pension that

National Debt

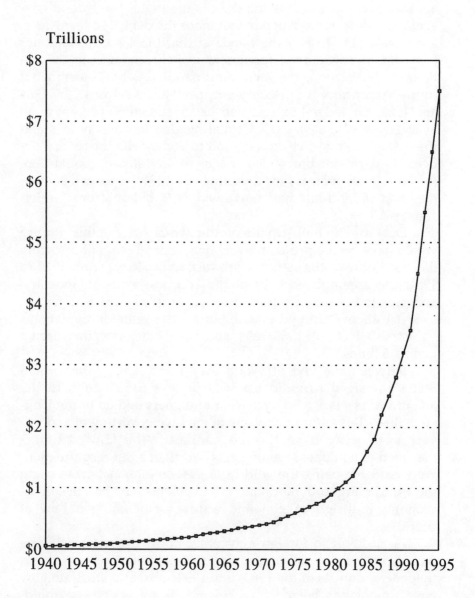

Source: Federal Reserve.

year, and it was more than six times the total spent on all education, job training, and unemployment programs.[4]

If we look back to the mid-1980s when the national debt was doubling, we can see the threefold economic consequences we are facing today. First, as the deficits mounted, the federal government needed to sell bonds to finance the debt. Too few Americans were able to buy the bonds at that time, so the Treasury Department encouraged foreigners to help underwrite the national debt. Second, the increasing national debt "encumbered future Americans by discouraging private investment. In 1984 and 1985, the federal budget deficits consumed 60 percent of all available private savings."[5] Capital needed to build homes and the nation's infrastructure was used to underwrite the federal deficit. Third, private borrowers looking for investment capital were forced to look overseas for financing. By 1984, American companies and individuals had borrowed $125 billion from foreign sources.[6]

Debt used to build up the productive capacity of this country would have been a prudent investment. But all of that borrowing did not improve the nation's productive capacity. From 1970 to 1984, the accumulated debt of the U.S. government, industry, and private households more than quadrupled from $1.6 trillion to $7.1 trillion. During the same period, the value of the nation's industries (steel mills, oil wells, automobile factories) increased a mere 1.6 times.[7]

Between the end of World War I and 1982, "the United States managed to build up a surplus of $152 billion in the amount of assets it held over what foreigners owned in the United States." But within two years of massive government and private borrowing from foreign sources, "the United States managed to liquidate seventy years' worth of asset accumulation. We went from being the world's largest creditor nation to being the world's largest debtor nation."[8] In essence, the nation sold its economic birthright of economic security for an indulgent bowl of porridge.

In addition to foreign debt obligations, domestic liabilities will also inevitably fall on the backs of baby boomers. Whereas the federal deficits of the 1980s and 1990s certainly illustrate how government has been living beyond its means, those mind-numbing numbers don't even begin to illustrate how many financial liabilities will accrue to the baby boom generation. Social Security and Medicare are two examples that we will discuss in

detail later in the chapter. Others include various federal entitlement programs, as well as governmental employee pensions. A
1985 estimate by the Treasury Department put the total liabilities
of all federal employee pension and disability plans at $1.2 trillion
(an amount comparable to the national debt at that time).[9]

The federal government is also the nation's largest insurer.
It insures loans to students, farmers, and small businessmen. It
insures bank deposits (as the S&L bailout reminds us), and it insures tens of millions of workers and retirees against the loss of
their private pensions. According to the Office of Management
and Budget, those future taxpayer liabilities exceed $3 trillion.[10]

So how large are the federal deficits? The answer is that they
are much larger than is publicly admitted. The figures are reported on a cash basis. But given the long-term liabilities, an accrual
method would more accurately reflect the long-term financial obligations.[11] Using accrual accounting Arthur Anderson found a
significant disparity between the government's cash-basis deficits
and the accounting firm's calculated accrual-bases deficit. The following chart for the budgets of 1974 and 1984 illustrates the substantial differences between the deficit figures when unfunded
liabilities are added to the calculations.[12]

Although those figures are discouraging, their impact will be
even more intense due to the demographics of the boomer generation. Paul Hewitt, of the Retirement Policy Institute, put it this
way:

> The baby boom as a generation has been its own worst enemy.
> Whenever we wanted anything the price went up, and when
> we sold the price went down. So we got less for our labor and
> paid more for our houses. When we want to sell those houses
> the price will go down, and when we want medical care in old
> age, prices will go up.[13]

As the pig in the python moves toward old age, the predictable
cycles of supply and demand will once again affect the boom
generation.

Many boomers are beginning to worry about such things as
whether they will financially be able to retire, whether there will
be any Social Security funds left for them, and who will take care
of them in their old age. While those are valid concerns, they are
easy to dismiss because they are still distant and long-term. But
boomers need not wait until the twenty-first century to begin

How Large is the Federal Deficit?
Comparison of Deficit Figures

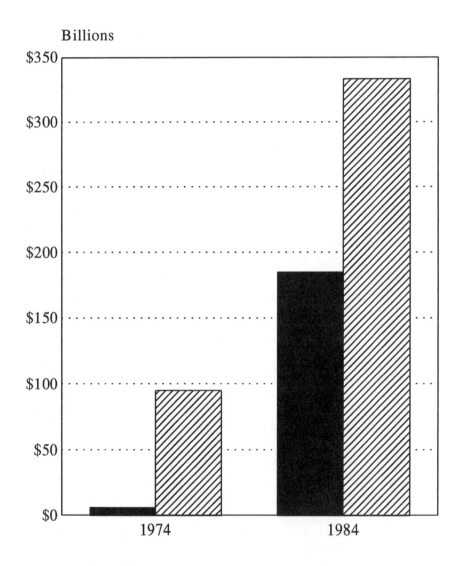

Billions

Cash-basis Accrual-basis

worrying. Many of them are facing a crisis in the 1990s that is already affecting their long-term financial security.

Boomers (specially those in the leading edge) have become "the triple-squeeze generation." The more than 25 percent of Americans between the ages of thirty-five and forty-four are finding their own retirement being squeezed out by the college costs of their children and the long-term healthcare costs of their aging parents. Sixty-six percent of baby boomers surveyed by the International Association of Financial Planning said "providing long-term care for a parent would affect their ability to save for their children's education" and would no doubt also affect their ability to save for their own retirement.[14]

If that is not difficult enough, consider the fact that this entire generation must also fund the retirement of the previous generation. Even if a baby boomer does not have the responsibility of caring for an aging parent, the entire generation must pay for the retirement and healthcare costs of the previous generation through Social Security and Medicare. In order to support themselves in their old age, baby boomers must do what no other generation has been forced to do: save for their own retirement while funding (at unprecedented levels) the retirement of the previous generation. The difficulty in doing this is that it forces many baby boomers to rethink their previous convictions about retirement.

RETHINKING RETIREMENT

Although the boom generation grew up assuming retirement (even early retirement) would be the norm, changing social and economic conditions may force a reevaluation of that assumption. After all, the idea of retirement itself is of recent origin.

When Social Security was first adopted in 1935, life expectancy was below sixty-three, a full two years under the retirement age.[15] Retirement was for the privileged few who lived long enough to enjoy the meager financial benefits from the system. In 1870, about 80 percent of men sixty-five and older worked.[16] Even as late as the 1950s, our contemporary image of retirement communities and the elderly sightseeing in recreational vehicles did not exist. Retirement was still nonexistent as an institution. Nearly half the men over age sixty-five were still in the work force.[17]

Today less than 15 percent of men over sixty-five are working, and the average age of retirement has plummeted to sixty.

Contrast that with the fact that the United States has become an aging society, thus extending the number of years of retirement and forcing individuals to save even more. Notice the remarkable change in the last fifty years alone. In 1940, an American at age twenty could expect to spend only 7 percent of his or her remaining life span in retirement. That number today has jumped to 23 percent, due to the twin factors of early retirement and increased life expectancy.[18]

Notice also the change in attitudes. Polls taken during the 1950s and early 1960s showed that most Americans desired to work for as long as they could and saw retirement merely for the disabled.[19] Today, however, most Americans look forward to their retirement as a time to travel, pursue personal interests, and generally indulge themselves. Unfortunately, the demographic landscape suggests that we may have to revise our current images of retirement.

As boomers slowly jog toward Golden Pond, they will likely be the largest generation of senior citizens in history: both in absolute size and in relative proportion to the younger generation. By the year 2000, the oldest boomers could be taking early retirement. The number of workers and dependents retired by 2025 could swell to as many as fifty-eight million workers and dependents, more than double the current number of retirees.[20]

In an effort to describe the uniqueness and enormity of this phenomenon, Ken Dychtwald calls this social tsunami the "Age Wave."

Three separate and unprecedented demographic phenomena are converging to produce the coming Age Wave.

The senior boom. Americans are living longer than ever before, and older Americans are healthier, more active, more vigorous, and more influential than any other generation in history.

The birth dearth. A decade ago, fertility in the United States plummeted to its lowest point ever. It has been hovering there ever since, and it's not likely to change. The great population of elders is not being offset by an explosion of children.

The aging of the baby boom. The leading edge of the boomer generation has now passed 40. As the boomers approach 50 and pass it, their numbers will combine with the other two great demographic changes to produce a historic shift in the concerns, structure, and style of America.[21]

Life Expectancy at Birth

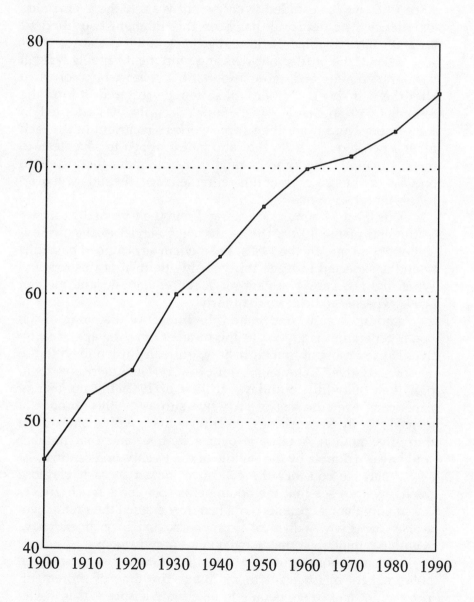

Source: U.S. Center for Health Statistics.

These phenomena, taken together, are certain to precipitate a "retirement crisis." First, people are living longer. In 1776, a child born in America could expect to live to age thirty-five. A century later, life expectancy was only forty.[22] In the decades since 1900, we have added twenty-eight years to the average life expectancy. The net result has been that in about two hundred years we have doubled the life expectancy in this country.[23]

Second, the burden of providing retirement benefits will fall upon the younger and, more important, smaller generation born after the baby boom. Never will so few be required to fund the retirement of so many. When Social Security was adopted in 1935, there were more than forty workers contributing to each federal pension. By 1950, the ratio had dropped to seventeen to one.[24] Currently the support ratio is a little more than three to one. When the last boomer hits retirement age, the ratio will drop to less than two to one.[25]

Third, baby boomers are aging. From the turn of the century to the end of the 1970s, the median age stayed in the twenty-something range. By the 1980s, the median age climbed past thirty and is expected to reach thirty-six by the turn of this century. When the last baby boomers reach retirement age, the median age is expected to be more than forty.

Another way to understand the impact of the aging of the boom generation is to look at the number over the age of sixty-five. During most of human history, only one in ten lived to the age of sixty-five. Today eight out of every ten Americans zoom past their sixty-fifth birthday.[26] In July of 1983, the number of Americans over the age of sixty-five surpassed the number of teenagers.[27] By the turn of the century, there will be more than thirty-five million Americans over sixty-five, and that number could nearly double by the middle of the twenty-first century.

When we consider the collective impact of each of those trends, we can see that the boom generation faces much greater uncertainty than its parents did when they entered their retirement years. That is why individuals, companies, and governments have begun to rethink their traditional notions of retirement.

William Johnston, of the Hudson Institute, has suggested that policymakers might want to rearrange the time of retirement. They might encourage people to take more leisure earlier in life, then work longer later or never really retire at all. Workers in their thirties or forties, for example, could be granted sabbaticals

Aging of America
Median Age of United States

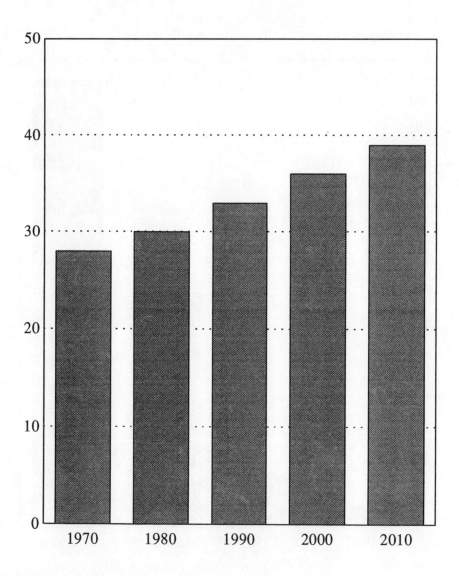

Source: U.S. Census Bureau.

Population Over Age 65
Actual and projected

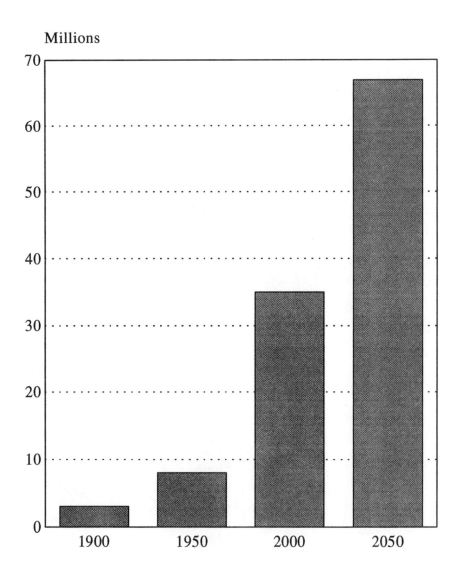

Millions

Source: U.S. Census Bureau.

to travel or rear children, drawing down some pension funds in exchange for working to age seventy or seventy-five.[28]

Some businesses, such as Macy's in New York or Tektronix in Oregon, do not have mandatory retirement policies. Hastings College of Law (University of California, Berkeley), has never had a mandatory retirement age and has long had a tradition of hiring older faculty who are retired from other institutions. A quarter of the faculty at Hastings is over sixty-five.[29]

Some companies, such as the Polaroid Company in Cambridge, Massachusetts, allow their employees leaves of absences before retirement, which are called "retirement rehearsals." If the transition to retirement is difficult, a person's job is still available to him or her.[30]

The members of the boom generation may even decide to reject the idea of retirement altogether, choosing instead to enrich themselves with meaningful work all of their lives. Yet such an idyllic vision could quickly be crushed by the harsh reality of failing health. Working until the age of seventy or beyond may not be physiologically possible for many people. Frances FitzGerald says, "Americans in their sixties and seventies are surely the first generation of healthy, economically independent retired people in history—and, in the absence of significant economic growth, they may well be the last."[31]

No wonder a chorus of Cassandras is predicting financial gloom in the next century. But significant changes can be made now to avert, or at least lessen, a potential crisis in the future. The future really depends on what the boom generation does in the 1990s to get ready for the "retirement century."

THE THREE-LEGGED STOOL

Twentieth-century Americans have always relied on a three-legged stool for their retirement—savings, pensions, and Social Security. Unfortunately, economic termites threaten the strength of that stool because boomers continue to spend rather than save, companies prune pensions, and Congress loots the Social Security trust fund.

BOOMER SAVINGS

The first leg on the retirement stool is savings. The boom generation is justly concerned about the savings (or lack of savings) it has put away so far for its retirement. A *Rolling Stone* survey in 1988 found that less than half of the leading edge baby boomers had been saving for retirement and less than a fourth of those under age thirty were saving for retirement.[32]

A survey by IDS Financial Services demonstrated the disparity between baby boomers' dreams and reality. They found that 97 percent of boomers said that ensuring a steady source of income at retirement is important, yet only half (53 percent) said they were doing very well or extremely well at retirement preparation. Why weren't they saving for retirement? Boomers said they were "too busy worrying about how to pay for their kids' education (37 percent), reducing credit burdens (36 percent), and making ends meet (35 percent)."[33]

This generation, therefore, is rightly concerned about its ability to save for its retirement. A survey of leading-edge boomers found that six out of ten expressed great concern about being able to meet all of their financial responsibilities, and 62 percent fear they will outlive their retirement savings.[34] But they aren't the only ones concerned. A survey by the American Academy of Actuaries echoed boomers' fears. Seventy-two percent of pension-fund actuaries polled predict that half of the baby boom won't have the wherewithal to retire at age sixty-five.[35]

Saving more is the obvious solution. Unfortunately, the United States has never been a nation of savers compared to the rest of the world. In 1988, for example, American households only saved 4.4 percent of their after-tax income. By contrast, the West Germans saved 12.6 percent, and the Japanese saved 15.2 percent.[36]

Already the baby boom generation itself is feeling the impact of this nation's meager savings rate. As this large generation entered the work force, it felt the impact of the lack of productive investment by its parents. According to economist Lester Thurow:

> The average American works with $58,000 (1982 dollars) worth of plant and equipment. To reach average productivity levels, new workers must be equipped with $58,000 worth of plant and equipment. Implicitly the parents of the baby boom generation were promising not just to bathe, feed, and educate their babies but to save $58,000 to equip each of their babies to enter the labor force twenty years later as the average American worker. And for every wife who entered the labor force the family was implicitly promising to save another $58,000. These implicit promises weren't kept.[37]

Savings for Retirement

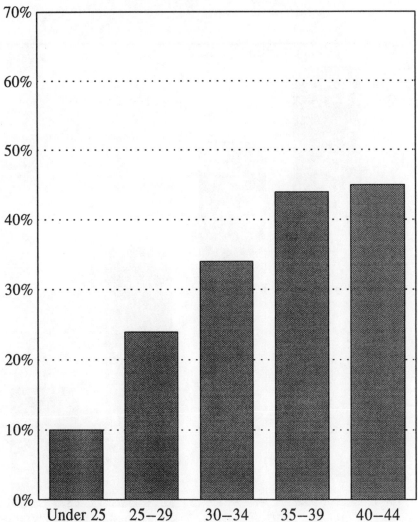

Percent of Boomers Saving

Source: Survey in *Rolling Stone* magazine (1988).

National Savings Rate
Net Household Savings as
Percent of Income after Taxes

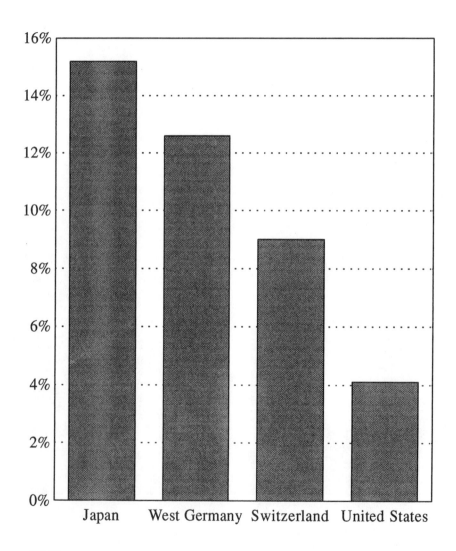

Source: OECD.

Not only has the saving rate been low; money that has been invested has not been put into productive investments. A large pool of savings could help build businesses and factories and re-build America's infrastructure. Unfortunately, a great deal of po-tential investment capital has gone to finance the sale and resale of houses with inflated prices. Compare a Japanese family to an American family. A typical Japanese family saves 21 percent of its disposable income and spends 5 percent on housing. By contrast, Americans save less than 6 percent and spend 15 percent on housing.[38]

When baby boomers entered the work force they managed to put even less money into savings than their parents did. In-stead, they went on a spending binge in the 1970s and 1980s. Some commentators have suggested that spending will now be replaced by a savings boom in the 1990s. So far there has not been a great deal of evidence for such a dramatic shift in consum-er behavior, however. If anything, the trends indicate that the rate of savings is down. A *Wall Street Journal*/NBC News poll in the late 1980s found that 55 percent of the leading-edge boomers surveyed said they were saving less than the year before. It also found that 50 percent of both the trailing edge and baby busters had also saved less.[39]

The surveys, however, are often subjective. A more telling statistic came from a survey designed to measure the amount of ready cash an individual or family had on hand. The survey asked whether the respondents could come up with $3,000 in a few days without borrowing or using a credit card. Of the lead-ing-edge boomers, 49 percent said they could and 49 percent said they couldn't. Not surprisingly a smaller percentage (only 29 per-cent) of the younger age groups had the $3,000.[40]

The inability of so many boomers to come up with the sum of $3,000 illustrates two things. First, it shows how little they have in savings or investments. Second, it demonstrates how deeply many of them are in debt. The first leg of the three-legged stool is in awful shape because, for many in the boom generation, savings are decreasing while debt is increasing.

Why are there such high levels of boomer debt? The reasons are fairly simple. First, members of the boom generation had great expectations for themselves and were often willing to go deeply into debt in order to finance the lifestyle they had chosen for themselves. Second, they had the misfortune of entering the consumer world at the time when wages were stagnant and when

Consumer Credit
for Selected Years

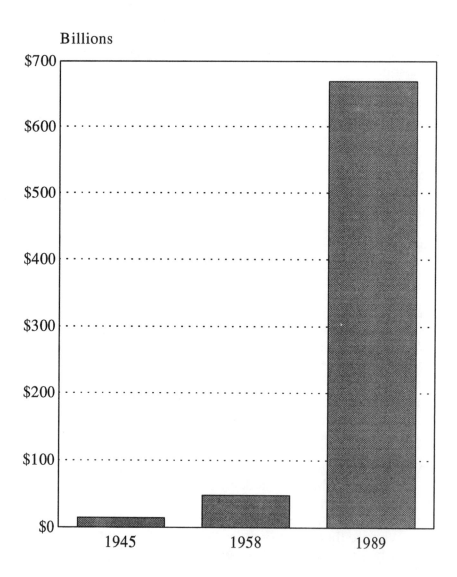

Source: American Demographics presentation.

most of the goods and services they craved were hit by inflation. Consumer borrowing was fueled, which became both a cause and a consequence of their downward mobility.

Between 1970 and 1983, the percentage of boomer families paying off consumer debt increased from two-thirds to three-fourths. Of families in debt in 1983, the average amount of debt was nearly $5,000.[41]

Families in debt usually are not saving. If they had any financial resources to save and invest, they would be wise to first retire their high-interest consumer debt. In 1984, more than a third of all households headed by a person under thirty-five had no savings whatsoever on deposit with banks and other financial institutions, aside from non-interest-paying checking accounts.[42]

In the midst of this dismal picture, some are still predicting a savings boom in the 1990s as boomers approach their peak saving years. Edward Yardeni, chief economist at Prudential-Bache Securities Inc., predicts that the boomers will increase the national savings rate to 10 percent by the mid-1990s. If he is correct, that would lift annual savings to $500 billion (compared with $147 billion in 1988).[43] His theory is simple. Forty-something boomers have already purchased the major items in their life: house, furnishing, family goods. And, he believes, because they have done most of their impulse buying, they are ready to settle down both socially and financially. In their earlier years, they went "out on the town." Now they prefer to lounge at home as "couch potatoes." As one boomer crassly put it, "I used to be a stud, now I'm a spud." Yardeni says, "The baby boomers who borrowed to buy houses in the '70s and '80s will be saving for retirement."[44]

Unfortunately, it is not that simple. Boomers have to make major adjustments to their lifestyle. Most of the boom generation has to get out of debt first. Then, they have to set out to save not just for retirement but also for their parents' healthcare and their children's college education.

Richard B. Berner, an analyst at Salomon Brothers, concedes that older boomers could nudge the savings level higher in the next few years. But he is much less sanguine about their impact, believing it will only increase the national savings rate by half a percentage point.[45] If he is right, the impact on the economy will be negligible because it will be offset by government "dissavings" (the budget deficit).

BOOMER PENSIONS

The second leg of the retirement stool is corporate pensions. In the past, there used to be an unwritten agreement between a company and an individual. If you faithfully worked for the company, the company would take care of you in your retirement. But that tacit agreement has broken down for two reasons.

First, many companies lack the financial resources to take care of the baby boom generation. Consolidation of some companies and the bankruptcy of others put pensions in jeopardy. Other companies that have had a measure of financial stability are beginning to feel the first financial tremors as the ratio of workers to retirees drops. In some older companies that offered generous retirement programs, the strains are already being felt. Bethlehem Steel Corporation, for example, had 33,000 active employees and nearly 70,000 retirees and surviving spouses.[46] Even companies with adequate financial resources will no doubt feel the financial ground shaking beneath them when the millions of baby boomers begin to retire.

Second, many baby boomers have not spent enough time with any one company to earn a significant pension. It was not uncommon for the parents of baby boomers to work for a single company for more than twenty years. Baby boomers, on the other hand, change jobs if not career paths with unprecedented frequency. Their apparent restlessness is born from both choice and necessity. Boomers are much less likely to stay in a job that does not enhance personal development and self-expression. Unlike their fathers who would often remain with a company "for the sake of the family," the boom generation is more likely to move on.

Boomers also change jobs out of necessity. They find themselves competing with each other for fewer upper-management positions for a number of reasons. First, companies thinned their management ranks. Most of that restructuring was done in the 1980s to make companies more efficient. The rest was a natural result of buyouts, takeovers, and consolidations leaving fewer structural layers in upper management and fewer jobs in general.

Second, boomers crowded into middle-management ranks at the same time restructuring was taking place. The leading-edge boomers in their prime career years are finding themselves on career "plateaus" and are becoming dissatisfied.

Third, there was a boom of business school graduates. The first boomers who graduated with MBAs were often ridiculed by classmates in other academic disciplines. But that initial condemnation gave way to active pursuit, and the number of business graduates quickly proliferated. As supply has outstripped demand, this ambitious group, with heightened expectations, finds itself frustrated and constantly looking for a job change.[47]

SOCIAL SECURITY

The third retirement leg was traditionally Social Security, but many boomers fear that Social Security will not be there for them when they retire, and for good reason. The demographics of the "Age Wave" will come crashing down upon the sandy foundations of the Social Security system.

When President Franklin Roosevelt designed the Social Security system, he and his advisers had many demographic variables working in their favor. As we have already mentioned, there were few old people, and life expectancy was age sixty-three.[48] On the other hand, there were many young people who could contribute to an old-age pension. So the Social Security Act worked very well in 1935 because it took a small contribution from a mass of young workers in order to provide meager benefits for a fraction of the retiring population. However, the demographic "Age Wave" threatens to turn the current system into nothing more than an elaborate Ponzi scheme.

Charles Ponzi was an Italian immigrant who developed a financial scheme in 1919 that seemed able to make him one of the wealthiest men in the world. He boldly announced to the world that using International Postal Union reply coupons he would take anyone's money and return a 50 percent profit in ninety days. As the money began to pour in, he surprised even skeptical investors by returning the money in just forty-five days. At that point, money poured into his investment scheme even faster than before.[49]

But soon, the investment bubble burst. Charles Ponzi began scrambling to pay back his early investors with money collected from his most recent investors. But there was simply not enough money. Like a person at the end of a chain letter or at the bottom of a marketing pyramid, there weren't enough people or enough dollars to make the scheme work. In the end, Ponzi was arrested, and investigators estimated assets of $4 million and liabilities of

$7 million, though no one knew for sure since he never kept any financial books.[50]

Critics of Social Security have often compared it to Ponzi's scheme because it does not invest the money but is a pay-as-you-go system that takes tax dollars from current workers to pay off previous contributors now eligible for benefits. Like Charles Ponzi, the Social Security system must have a larger base of contributors than recipients. Clearly that will not be the case in the future due to the "senior boom" and the "birth dearth."

Advances in modern medicine have raised life expectancy by twenty-eight years in this century alone. The median age is headed toward forty, and some demographers see the median age reaching as high as fifty years old. One has to wonder about the stability of Social Security in a country where half of the people qualify for membership in the American Association of Retired Persons.[51]

But median age is only one indicator of the potential crisis. In 1935, those who lived to be age sixty-five could only expect to live a few more years. Not only are more people reaching age sixty-five than ever before, many who reach that age can expect to live not just a few years more, but a few decades more!

One of the most popular features on NBC's "Today" show has been Willard Scott's greeting to those Americans age 100 or older. Those who watch the program assume that he is greeting all those who have passed the century mark, but that is hardly the case. The U.S. Census Bureau recorded 35,808 centenarians in 1990.[52] That is twice the number just a decade before. In order to cover the country, Willard Scott would have to list 100 centenarians a day on the broadcast.

The demands placed on Social Security by the senior boom will be significant. Some people will be receiving benefits for almost as many years as they paid into the system. That is especially sobering when considering that these people will be receiving benefits adjusted for cost of living (COLAs).

A second concern is the ratio between generations. President Roosevelt established the Social Security when there were masses of young people who could be called upon to support the elderly in poverty. Even though implemented during the Depression when many were out of work, the ratio of workers to recipients was substantial. If you retired in 1935, more than 40 workers were contributing to your pension. Those who retired in 1990 had only 3.4 workers supporting their pension. According

Centenarians

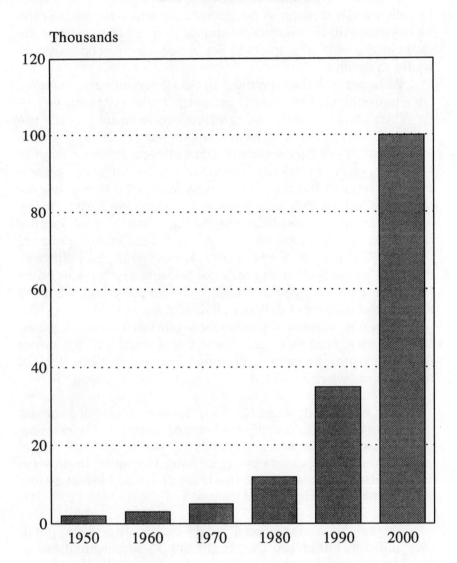

Thousands

Source: Census Bureau.

to economist Richard Rahn, that support ratio could drop to 1.78 to 1 by the year 2020.[53]

The smaller generation following the boom generation will be called upon to support Social Security when boomers retire. The system will face incredible strains through the next few decades as the ratio of workers to Social Security beneficiaries continues to decline.

Although the demographics of Social Security are ominous, equally troubling concerns surface in the politics of Social Security. When Congress increased contributions to Social Security under the Federal Insurance Contributions Act (FICA) in the early 1980s, part of the funds went to a Social Security Trust Fund to build up a reserve of as much as $12 trillion for the boom generation's retirement. But those funds have been used to disguise the size of the federal deficit. In other words, other parts of the federal government are essentially writing IOUs to the Social Security trust fund. Donald Leavens, director of federal budget policy at the U.S. Chamber of Commerce, warns: "What the politicians don't tell you is that when the Social Security system goes broke in 2018, the government is going to have to pony up the money for all those trillions of dollars in IOUs."[54]

Although various administration officials have maintained that the trust fund is secure, their claims could not be further from the truth. Economic columnist Warren Brookes did not mince words when he stated:

> Let's be perfectly clear: The Social Security Trust Funds do not now nor have they ever really existed, except as bookkeeping entries. Even the notes and bonds . . . don't exist except as serial numbers on a computer. In order to convert those serial numbers into real money, the Treasury would have to go into the market and borrow.[55]

The solutions to the Social Security crisis are few and politically difficult. Either you change the supply of contributions or the demand of the recipients. Increasing the supply of contributors could be achieved by increasing the birth rate (unlikely, and probably too late) or allowing more immigration of workers who could contribute to Social Security. Substantial economic growth would be another way to increase the amount of contributions, but the amount of economic growth necessary for the system to

Social Security
Ratio of Workers to Recipients

Number of workers supporting pension

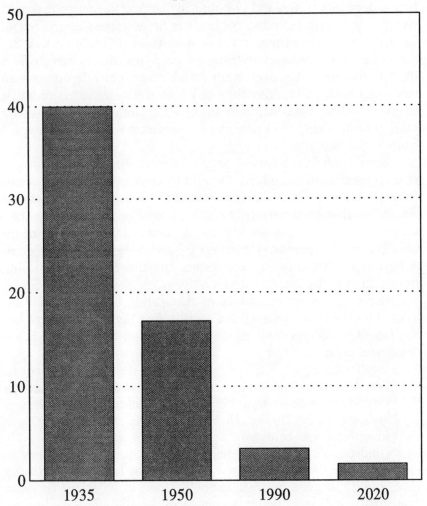

Source: Age Wave

work exceeds any reasonable assumption of future GNP growth in this country.[56]

Another way to increase the supply of contributions is to increase FICA payments. But there will be an upper limit on how much Americans can be taxed. If benefits stay at their current levels, workers in 2040 could find Social Security taking as much as 40 percent of their paychecks.[57]

If increasing the supply of contributions is economically difficult, decreasing demand is politically difficult because it would require trimming benefits. So far, the beneficiaries of the Social Security system are the current recipients. A retiree on Social Security today recovers everything he paid into the system in less than two years.[58] On the other hand, most baby boomers will never get back the money they pay into the system.[59] Economist Michael Boskin has concluded studies that under current law, the younger one's age, the lower the rate of return one should expect from Social Security.[60]

Some politicians have suggested trimming benefits to current recipients. Although that would be difficult to achieve politically, it makes good sense economically. An estimated 500,000 to 600,000 millionaires currently receive Social Security payments.[61] Whereas those people are the exceptions, the staggering numbers indicate the reasonableness of applying a means test to Americans with considerable assets. In the future, politicians must explain why cashiers and factory workers have to pay Social Security benefits to hundreds of thousands of retired millionaires. Questions of generational equity and social justice are being raised by liberals and conservatives alike. Economist Milton Friedman says:

> Social Security has helped the wealthy much more than the poor. On the one hand, the relatively well-to-do have a longer life expectancy. On the other hand, they tend to enter the work force later and contribute to the fund for a shorter time. My children, for instance, entered the work force after college in their twenties. A kid from a working-class family, if he's lucky enough to get a job, will enter the force at 15 or 16. This bias greatly overweighs the payout formulae that are weighted toward the poor.[62]

If Congress does not trim current benefits, it will most likely be forced to trim future benefits to the baby boom generation.

Congress has already increased the age of retirement and may induce workers to stay on the job until age seventy. Another solution would be to provide bigger tax breaks for workers to fund their own retirement through IRAs, Keogh, and so on.

A FOURTH LEG

Savings, pensions, or Social Security have traditionally been seen as the three legs of the retirement stool. But a vital fourth leg has recently been added: health insurance. Healthcare costs have been steadily increasing, especially since the mid-1950s. But this crisis has intensified due, once again, to the senior boom. An aging population in America increases the demands for healthcare due to the simple fact that older people, generally, require more healthcare than do the young. Approximately one-third of all healthcare spending in the United States is consumed by those over age sixty-five.[63]

One of the ironies of healthcare is that although medical advances allow more and more Americans to reach advancing age, that increases the probability of contracting a long and debilitating illness. Put another way, medicine has often been more successful at extending the quantity of life than in improving the quality of life. Extending the average age has increased the chance of coming down with an illness or physical condition that is so expensive as to be beyond what a person or family could afford on their own.

Future retirees may be hit harder by two trends going in opposite directions. The cost of healthcare (when measured as a percentage of this nation's Gross National Product) has doubled in less than thirty years and continues to rise. While the cost of healthcare is rising, the amount of health-insurance coverage is declining (as healthcare premiums soar 10 to 20 percent).[64]

For years, medical care and insurance was a neglected area of political discussion, yet this has changed significantly in the 1990s. The trust fund for Medicare is in worse shape than Social Security, and by the early part of the twenty-first century Medicare will surpass Social Security as the largest domestic program.[65]

Healthcare has already become the new battleground over entitlement programs. Medicare distributes scarce financial resources on the basis of seniority, and many in our society are likely to challenge the justification for that allocation. Nearly one-third of all Medicare dollars go to patients who die within a

Healthcare Costs

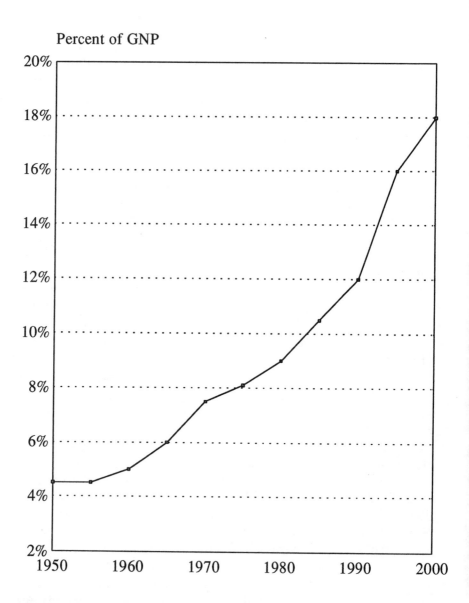

Percent of GNP

Source: Office of National Health Statistics.

year.[66] Often that allocation is made at the expense of the young and healthy.

> In the early 1980s, many states tightened their Medicaid eligibility requirements for children and young women. As a result, infant mortality rates have soared in many communities. Obviously, those infants who are dying have no chance at becoming senior citizens. But the great irony is that, under our current laws, if they had somehow managed to survive to age sixty-five, society would have spared virtually no expense in prolonging their lives a few more years.[67]

Pressures on the private sector will also be intense. Companies already feeling the financial pressure from corporate pensions will feel additional pressure from corporate healthcare plans. In the mid-1980s, the unfunded, postemployment healthcare liability of the Fortune 500 companies approached $2 trillion, whereas the total assets of those companies were only $1.4 trillion.[68]

As health costs escalate and coverage shrinks, healthcare reform becomes mandatory. The possible proposals range from providing tax incentives for private insurance plans to a nationalized healthcare system. But the broader question of whether seniority is an adequate justification for scarce healthcare resources is sure to surface.

POLITICS OF AGING

The potential for inter-generational warfare is great. In the next century, aging baby boomers will most likely be lobbying for healthcare programs that support long-term medical and home healthcare. Members of the younger generation, on the other hand, will probably be lobbying for more support for prenatal and genetic screening to protect their offspring from various illnesses.[69] Similar battles are likely to break out over tax incentives, savings programs, pension programs, and especially Social Security.

The boom generation profoundly affected American society in its youth. Moreover, its ability to influence and alter the direction of society in the middle-aged and elderly years will be even more significant. Their influence is being felt in the presidential elections, and they will continue to be a force to acknowledge and appease. When they reach old age, their influence will be substantial. Already the American Association for Retired Persons (AARP) is the largest political lobby in the country, twice the size of the AFL-CIO.[70] Organizations such as Americans for Generational Equity (AGE) and the American Association of Boomers have been formed to lobby for the interests of boomers. Phillip Longman, author of *Born to Pay*, sees the boom generation taking an active political role in the future.

> So long as democratic institutions survive, the baby boomers will enjoy great political strength in old age. Politicians will bid against one another to court their vote. Entrepreneurs will organize vast pressure groups to lobby on their behalf. The baby boomers are sure to find their own curmudgeonly "spokesperson" to play the role of Claude Pepper. But while the baby boomers in old age will command far more votes and probably will enjoy far greater political influence than do today's senior citizens, they will nonetheless be forced to seek their support from a working-aged population that will be comparatively much smaller and quite likely poorer.[71]

No doubt they will face more difficult demographic and economic circumstances than their parents faced in their old age. Boomers will have to be supported by a smaller generation and by a governmental system that will be straining to provide even meager assistance.

They will also face a more difficult political situation. The federal government will no doubt be less able, and certainly less willing, to fund entitlement programs in the twenty-first century.

> Millions of people have been able to go to college and buy homes because a kindly Uncle Sam co-signed the loans. Millions have slept soundly at night because of Uncle's pledge that their savings are in fact safe. And when more than half a million people wanted to launch businesses no private lender could help, Uncle was there. But now, burned by the estimated $500 billion it will cost to solve the savings-and-loan crisis, Uncle Sam may have to become Uncle Scrooge.[72]

The boom generation does indeed face a crisis of security and will soon be asking the question, Who will care for me? In the past, children have cared for their parents in their old age. But as many as 20 percent of baby boomers do not have children. For the rest that do, children may not be enough. Their children may be unable, or (even more chilling) may be unwilling to care for them. If that is the case, then the boom generation will have to depend on the three- or four-legged stool for retirement. The personal and political choices they make now will determine how stable the stool will be by the time they retire.

NOTES

1. U.S. Bureau of the Census, *Historical Statistics of the United States* and *Statistical Abstract of the United States.*
2. Bob Rast, "Baby Boomers Predict Hard Times in the 90s," *Dallas Times Herald,* 16 June 1990, B-1.
3. It took 205 years for the federal deficit to reach $1 trillion and only five years for it to reach $2 trillion.
4. Office of Management and Budget, *Special Analyses,* E-12, table E-5.
5. Phillip Longman, *Born to Pay: The New Politics of Aging in America* (Boston: Houghton Mifflin, 1987), 24.
6. Barry P. Bosworth, "Fiscal Fitness: Deficit Reduction and the Economy," *Brookings Review,* Winter-Spring 1986, 3.
7. U.S. Bureau of the Census, *Statistical Abstract of the United States: 1986* (Washington, D.C.: U.S. Government Printing Office, 1985), tables 817, 897.
8. Longman, *Born to Pay,* 26.
9. Treasury Department, Financial Management Service, *Consolidated Financial Statements of the United States Government: Fiscal Year 1985, Prototype* (Washington, D.C.: U.S. Government Printing Office, 1986), 27.
10. Longman, *Born to Pay,* 196.
11. Accrual accounting puts liabilities down as they are accrued rather than when they are paid off. Those figures then reflect both the financial obligations as well as the interest costs into the future.
12. *Sound Financial Reporting in the U.S. Government: A Prerequisite to Fiscal Responsibility,* Arthur Anderson, 1986.
13. David Kirkpatrick, "Will You Be Able to Retire?" *Fortune,* 31 July 1989, 57.
14. Rast, "Baby Boomers."
15. Landon Jones, *Great Expectations: America and the Baby Boom Generation* (New York: Ballantine, 1980), 375.
16. Ken Dychtwald and Joe Flower, *Age Wave: The Challenges and Opportunities of an Aging America* (New York: Bantam, 1990), 118.
17. U.S. Bureau of Labor Statistics, *Recent Trends in Labor Force Participation Rates: A Chartbook* (Washington, D.C.: U.S. Government Printing Office, 1980).
18. Barbara Boyle Torrey, "The Lengthening of Retirement," in *Aging from Birth to Death,* vol. 2, ed. Matilda White Riley et al. American Association for the Advancement of Science, Selected Symposium no. 79.
19. Philip Ash, "Pre-retirement Counseling," *The Gerontologist,* June 1967, 97-99.
20. Susan Dentzer, "How We Will Live," *U.S. News and World Report,* 25 December 1989, 62.

21. Dychtwald and Flower, *Age Wave*, 4.
22. Ibid.
23. Ibid., 6.
24. Ibid., 68.
25. Kirkpatrick, "Will You Be Able to Retire?" 56.
26. David Gergen, "Sixtysomething: Part 1," *U.S. News and World Report*, 16 April 1990, 64.
27. Dychtwald and Flower, *Age Wave*, 8.
28. Dentzer, "How We Will Live," 64.
29. Dychtwald and Flower, *Age Wave*, 182.
30. Ibid., 193.
31. Francis FitzGerald, *Cities on a Hill: A Journey Through Contemporary American Cultures* (New York: Simon & Schuster, 1986), 209.
32. William Greider, "Money Matters," *Rolling Stone*, 7 April 1988, 48.
33. Eric Miller and Research Alert editors, *Future Vision: The 189 Most Important Trends of the 1990s* (Naperville, Ill.: Sourcebooks Trade, 1991), 95.
34. Rast, "Baby Boomers," B-1.
35. Dentzer, "How We Will Live," 62.
36. Rich Thomas, "Saving: Not the American Way," *Newsweek*, 8 January 1990, 44.
37. Lester Thurow, *The Zero-Sum Solution: Building a World-Class American Economy* (New York: Simon & Schuster, 1985), 84.
38. Kenneth T. Jackson, *Crabgrass Frontier: The Suburbanization of the United States* (New York: Oxford Univ., 1985), 295.
39. Ibid.
40. Ibid.
41. Statistics from Robert Avery et al., "Survey of Consumer Finances, 1983: A Second Report," *Federal Reserve Bulletin* (December 1984) and Frank Levy and Richard Michel, "The Economic Future of the Baby Boom," paper presented at conference for Americans for Generational Equity, 10 April 1986.
42. U.S. Bureau of the Census, Current Population Reports, *Household Wealth and Asset Ownership: 1984*, series P-70, no. 7, 8.
43. Pamela Sebastian, "Baby Boomers," *Wall Street Journal*, 13 February 1989, A-1.
44. Thomas, "Saving," 44.
45. Sebastian, "Baby Boomers," A-1.
46. Dychtwald and Flower, *Age Wave*, 83.
47. "Career-Stalled Boomers May Advance 'Sideways,'" *The Boomer Report*, 15 June 1990, 6.
48. Dychtwald and Flower, *Age Wave*, 66.
49. Longman, *Born to Pay*, 64.
50. "Ponzi Dies in Brazil," *Life*, 31 January 1949, 63.
51. Jim Wright, "Learning to Surf on the Age Wave," *Dallas Morning News*, 19 February 1989, 39A.
52. Melinda Beck, "Attention, Willard Scott," *Newsweek*, 4 May 1992, 75.
53. Quoted in Dychtwald and Flower, *Age Wave*, 68.
54. Donald Leavens, "How Much Are You Overpaying for Social Security?" *Human Events*, 13 January 1990, 15.
55. Column by Warren Brookes, 11 February 1990, distributed by Creators Syndicate, Inc.

56. The Social Security Administration estimates that real wages must double over current levels by 2015 and increase sixfold before 2060 in order to provide for the baby boom generation. This estimate also assumes that fertility rates increase rapidly as well. Social Security Administration, *The 1986 Annual Report of the Board of Trustees of the Federal Old-Age and Survivors Insurance and Disability Insurance Trust Funds* (Washington, D.C.: U.S. Government Printing Office, 1986).

57. Kirkpatrick, "Will You Be Able to Retire?" 59.

58. A married worker retiring at age sixty-five who paid the maximum amount of Social Security taxes would recover his or her contributions in just twenty-one months. Low wage earners would recover their contributions in as little as twelve months. Geoffrey Kollman and David Koitz, "How Long Does It Take for New Retirees to Recover the Value of the Social Security Taxes?" Congressional Research Service, 21 January 1986, report no. 86-10, 11.

59. One study demonstrated that all baby boomers who remain single throughout their lifetimes, except women who earn no more than $10,000 a year, will be net losers. It also found that all two-paycheck families with incomes higher than $20,000 (the typical baby boom family) will likewise pay more in taxes than they receive in benefits. Anthony Pellechio and Gordon Goodfellow, "Individual Gains and Losses from Social Security Before and After the 1983 Amendments," *Cato Journal*, Fall 1983, 417–42.

60. Michael J. Boskin, *Too Many Promises: The Uncertain Future of Social Security* (Honeywood, Ill.: Dow Jones-Irwin, 1986).

61. Dychtwald and Flower, *Age Wave*, 74.

62. Ibid., 201.

63. House Committee on Ways and Means, *Background Information on Programs Under the Jurisdiction of the Committee on Ways and Means*, 99th Congress, 1st sess., 1985.

64. "As Baby Boomers Age, More Worry About Health Care," *Dallas Morning News*, 24 November 1989, 58A.

65. Ibid.

66. Victor R. Fuchs, "'Though Much is Taken': Reflections on Aging, Health and Medical Care," *Milbank Memorial Quarterly/Health and Society*, Spring 1984, 164–65.

67. Longman, *Born to Pay*, 116.

68. Joseph Califano, Jr., *America's Health Care Revolution* (New York: Random House, 1986), 14, 30.

69. Robert Kubey, "Aging Boomer May Battle Young for Fair Share," *Dallas Times Herald*, 2 January 1989, C-3.

70. Kubey, "Aging Boomer May Battle," C-1.

71. Longman, *Born to Pay*, 8.

72. Bill Montague, "Credit Crises Set Stage for Debt Debate," *USA Today*, 10 September 1990, B-1.

CHAPTER TEN
THE CRISIS OF SPIRITUALITY

T he last thing on Bill's mind when he caught the 7:05 flight was religion. But somehow during the trip he got into a interesting discussion with the man sitting next to him on the plane—John. An hour into the conversation, Bill asked John what he did for a living. When John said he was a Baptist minister, Bill almost jumped out of his seat!

Bill grew up in a Catholic home and attended Mass on a fairly regular basis. During grade school he went to catechism and stayed involved with the church through part of his teen years. By the time he went off to college, though, he had essentially left the Catholic church.

Occasionally during his college years he came back to religious questions. One time Bill visited a charismatic church with a friend. Another time he signed up to do Transcendental Meditation. Sometimes he even took time to debate with some of the members of the local campus Christian group that came to witness in the student union.

By the time Bill headed out into the corporate world he had shoved spiritual issues to the back burner. He needed to be successful in his new job, and religion didn't seem relevant or important. Nevertheless, Bill felt an emptiness in his life that could not be filled with things such as money or success. He wondered if he should return to his religious roots, especially now that his toddlers were nearing school-age.

Sitting next to John reopened all of those questions and concerns. As they talked, Bill was surprised by the depth of his own curiosity about religious things. Here was someone he could talk to about an area of his life that was much more important than even he realized. Questions about the Bible, Christianity, churches, denominations came pouring out. Soon the two men were engaged in an intense conversation about spiritual issues that lasted until the flight landed. As they exchanged business cards and phone numbers, Bill knew that a new journey in his life was about to begin as he and his wife began the process of finding a church home.

Bill's spiritual journey matches the religious pilgrimage of many of his fellow baby boomers. They grew up in religious households (96 percent) but jettisoned their beliefs when they became adults because spirituality seemed irrelevant in the secular, pluralistic culture of modern life.[1]

The process of secularization in modern society removed religious ideas and institutions from the dominant place they had in previous generations. Religious ideas were less meaningful, and religious institutions more marginal in their influence on the baby boom generation.[2] To their parents' dismay, most boomers (58 percent) dropped out of traditional religion for at least two years during their adolescence and adulthood.[3]

The process of pluralization in their world rapidly multiplied the number of worldviews, faiths, and ideologies. As we noted in the chapter on priorities, that increase in choice led naturally to a decrease in commitment and continuity.[4] Many boomers during their adolescence and early adulthood went through what might be best called serial conversions. Spiritually hungry for meaning, they dined heartily at America's cafeteria for alternative religions: est, gestalt, meditation, scientology, bioenergetics, and the New Age. Others sought spiritual peace through twelve-step programs for alcoholics, workaholics, even chocoholics. Such have-it-your-way, salad-bar spirituality has been high on choices and options but low on spiritual commitment.

Survey of Religious Attitudes in America

- 94% believe in God
- 92% state a religious preference
- 90% pray
- 88% believe God loves them
- 78% say they have given "a lot" or "a fair amount" of thought to their relationship with God over the past two years
- 68% say they are members of a church or synagogue
- 56% say religion is "very important" in their lives
- 40% attend church or synagogue in a given week

Source: George Gallup and Jim Castelli, *The People's Religion*, 1989.

The bewildering array of spiritualities in this country easily blends into a nice bland pablum that goes down without any problem. Although there are those who try to follow the demanding precepts of traditional religion, most baby boomers find refreshment in a vague religiosity which does not interfere in any way with how they live.[5]

As this generation passes through midlife, it will inevitably look to the future with more anxiety than anticipation. Boomers are asking, Who will care for me? Will I be able to provide for myself and my family? And those questions are also mingled with questions of identity. Who am I? Where am I going? Is this all there is to life? The questions have an underlying spiritual dimension and are not easily answered in a secular world nor in a mystical world filled with bland spirituality.

Certainly this generation has sought answers in self-help programs and community activities, but something more than social changes and technology is necessary. As one commentator said, "There is a feeling of being lost and looking for something greater. People know that technology hasn't worked for them. It hasn't done anything for their souls."[6]

SEEKERS OF SPIRITUALITY

As in other endeavors, baby boomers have been seekers: seekers of pleasure, seekers of experience, seekers of freedom, seekers of wealth, and, yes, seekers of spirituality. But unlike their parents, boomers took unpredictable paths in their search for spirituality. This generation has been eclectic in its religious experiences where brand loyalty is unheard of and the customer is king. Although some have stayed true to the "faith of their fathers," most mix traditional religion with New Age mysticism and modern self-help psychologies in a flexible and syncretistic manner.

Tracking this generation's values and attitudes toward religion and spiritual issues is not easy, if for no other reason than the lack of substantial research. Most of the significant research on boomer attitudes toward religion has been done within the last ten years. Consider this comment from the late 1980s:

> When the first of its number reached 40 last summer, the Baby Boom once again entered the spotlight. But for all the coverage, including a 10-page cover story in *Time* and [Landon] Jones' 350-page book, little more than a paragraph was written on the role of religion in the lives of the Baby Boom generation.[7]

Fortunately more data since then has provided a better perspective on this generation's attitudes and perspectives on religion.

Boomers may be divided into three religious subcultures: loyalists, returnees, and dropouts.[8] Loyalists tend to be social conservatives. They had good relationships with their parents and tended to grow up in strict homes. Loyalists never really identified with the counterculture and never left church or synagogue.

At the other extreme are the dropouts. They had less confidence in the country when growing up and had more conflicts with their parents. Traditional religion was, to them, out of touch with modern life. They have never come back to church and pursue spirituality (if at all) in a personal and individual way.

Between the loyalists and the dropouts are the returnees. They were and are middle-of-the-road types who were less alienated than the dropouts but more disaffected than the loyalists. They left church or synagogue and have returned, but often with some ambivalence.

Spiritual Beliefs
Percent of Baby Boomers by Religious Involvement and Spiritual Beliefs

	Loyalists	Returnees	Dropouts
Believe "God is within us"	16	20	49
Read the Bible	76	76	38
Believe in astrology	20	20	36
Believe in reincarnation	19	23	36
Practice daily prayer	72	72	30
Practice meditation	12	13	16
Say grace	58	54	13

Source: Wade Clark Roof, "The Baby Boom's Search for God," *American Demographics*, 1992.

Each religious subculture manifests differences in spiritual styles and commitment, but all are affected to some degree by their experiences in the counterculture. Though their views are different from one another, collectively the three boomer subcultures are very different from their parents. For example, few members of the returnees subculture actually consider themselves religious or hold to traditional views of God, even though they may actually attend religious services on a regular basis. Returnees are much less likely to engage in traditional religious activities (daily prayers, saying grace at meals, reading the Bible). Almost one-fourth of returnees (23 percent) and nearly one-fifth of loyalists (19 percent) say they believe in reincarnation. Twenty percent of churchgoing returnees question how important church services are and even go so far as to say that since "people have God within them, churches aren't necessary."[9]

RETURN TO CHURCH

Those who have returned to church—the so-called "baby boomerangs"—have returned for one of two major reasons: children or spiritual restlessness. Boomers concerned about the moral and spiritual upbringing of their children have made the spiritual pilgrimage back to their religious roots. Members of this generation may say they do not believe in absolute values, but frequently their relativistic worldview collapses when they have children. They don't want their kids growing up without any moral direction, so church suddenly becomes a much more important place. Gallup surveys, for example, show that nearly nine in ten Americans say they want religious training for their kids, even though fewer than seven in ten with children (ages four to eighteen) say they are currently providing such training. [10]

The boomerang phenomenon is not peculiar to baby boomers. Church historians have found a predictable pattern of church attendance that has affected numerous generations. Typically after high school, young adults drop out of church and often don't drop back into church until they have children. In that regard, boomers are no different than generations that preceded them.

Unlike previous generations, however, boomers have prolonged the cycle by postponing marriage and parenthood. Getting married later and having children later essentially extended their absence from church. And that extended absence allowed many of them to get more set in their ways. A generation used to free weekends and sleeping in on Sunday is less likely to make church attendance a priority.

Kids begin to rearrange those priorities. Statistically, it has been shown that the presence of children in a family makes a significant difference in the likelihood of church attendance. One survey found that married baby boomers are nearly three times more likely to return to church if they have children (50 percent to 18 percent). [11] Children do indeed seem to be leading their parents back to church.

Another reason for boomers' return to church is spiritual restlessness. Sixteen hundred years ago, Saint Augustine acknowledged, "We were made for thee, O God, and our hearts are restless until they find rest in thee." Social commentators have generally underestimated the impact of this generation's restless desire for meaning and significance. Ken Woodward, religion editor for *Newsweek*, stated, "That search for meaning is a powerful motivation to return to the pews. In the throes of a midlife re-evaluation, Ecclesiastes—'A time for everything under heaven'—is suddenly relevant." [12] George Gallup has found that two-thirds of those who dropped out of a traditional church for two years or more returned because they "felt an inner need" to go back and rediscover their religious faith. [13]

Church Attendance
for Married Baby Boomers

Percent of Dropout Boomers Who
Returned or Remained Dropouts

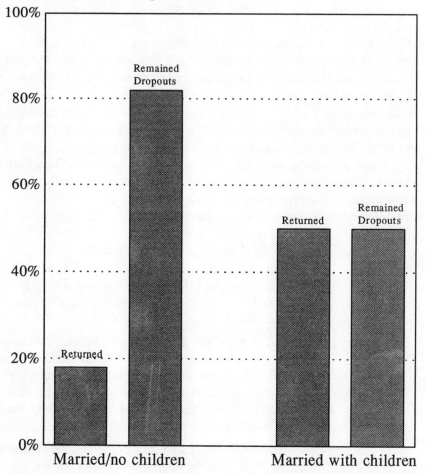

Household Composition

Source: Roof survey in American Demographics (1992)

For those and other less significant reasons, baby boomers are returning to church, though not in the numbers sometimes reported in the media. All of this attention to returning boomers fails to take into account that more than 40 percent of baby boomers have not returned to church.[14] Spiritual interest has not always translated into church attendance. And when boomers do attend church it is on an irregular basis. "According to a survey by *People* magazine, baby boomers go to church an average of about six times a year—less than half as often as Americans over forty."[15]

That lack of church attendance was somewhat of a surprise, not only to social commentators but to baby boomers themselves. When *Rolling Stone* magazine commissioned a survey of boomer attitudes toward various institutions, it uncovered some surprising changes in attitudes. Boomers found themselves to be more family-oriented, more conservative, and more career-oriented than they anticipated when they were younger. However, 50 percent said they were less involved in organized religion than they expected they would be when they were younger.[16]

Evidently the skepticism this age group has toward all institutions (government, military, schools) also appears in their attitude toward church. Although they are consistent with previous generations in their boomerang cycle, "statistics on church attendance, when viewed up close, reveal dramatic and distinctive patterns along generational lines."[17] The data show:

- Throughout their lives, Americans born during the Depression [born in 1930s] have been more faithful than later generations in their church/synagogue attendance.

- "War babies" [born 1919–45] dropped out of church as they entered their twenties during the turbulent sixties, and stayed away. The twin disillusionments stemming from Vietnam and Watergate made them more suspicious of institutions—the church included. Only as they approach and pass midlife are they trickling back to church.

- Baby boomers [born 1946–64] also dropped out of the church in their twenties, but now, in their thirties and forties, they are returning to the ranks of the faithful. The real boom in church attendance is coming from this generation.[18]

Nevertheless, boomers are returning to church in increasing numbers. By the early 1980s the number of leading edge baby

Organized Religion

Compared with how you thought you would turn out as an adult, are you more or less . . .

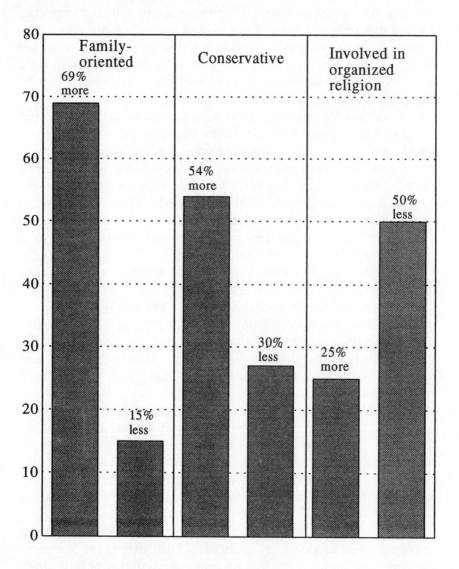

boomers who attend church regularly rose nearly 10 percentage points (from 33.5 percent to 42.8 percent) and continued to rise through the decade.[19]

Will that revitalized interest in religion make a difference in society? It is a question many social commentators are considering. "Will the churches and synagogues provide the kind of training necessary to keep the faith vital—or will the churches merely mirror the culture?" asks sociologist Os Guinness. "The natural tendency of the baby boomers is to be laissez faire socially. Will their return to faith make any decisive difference in their personal and social ethics, or will their religious commitment be [simply] a variant of their social philosophy?"[20]

Traditionally boomers have been samplers with little brand loyalty. They don't feel bound to the denomination of their youth, and they search for experiences (both spiritual and otherwise) that meet their needs. It is not uncommon for families to attend different churches each week (sometimes on the same day) to meet their perceived spiritual needs. They aren't bashful about attending a particular church to take advantage of a special seminar or program and then picking up and moving to another church when its programs seem inviting.

Many boomers may be interested in spiritual issues but see no need to attend church. George Gallup refers to that as "The Unchurched in America—Faith Without Fellowship." Religious individualism stems both from American individualism that has been a part of this country for centuries and this generation's desire for flexibility and individuality. The have-it-your-way attitude in every area of a boomer's life has given rise to such religious individualism.

Statistical validation of this perceived religious individualism came from a survey of the readers of *Better Homes and Gardens*. The survey found that nearly three-fourths (74 percent) believe it is possible to be a moral person without being a spiritual person. And a majority (52 percent agree, 34 percent disagree) believe that it is possible to be a spiritual person without being religious.[21]

Boomers approach religion and spirituality differently from previous generations. They embrace a faith that is low on commitment and high on choice. As one commentator noted, "they are comfortable with a vague, elastic faith that expands to fill the world after a pleasant Christmas service and contracts to nothing when confronted with difficulties."[22] No wonder many boomers are starting to embrace a religious faith that previous generations would never have considered.

THE NEW AGE MOVEMENT

One of the most intriguing religious trends in the last few decades has been the phenomenal growth of what has come to be called the New Age movement. Even with the proliferation of Eastern philosophies in the 1960s, it is nevertheless surprising that the New Age has grown to such proportions.

The growing secularization of society seemed to point to a more secular world that is hostile to religion. The rise and growth of the New Age certainly would not have been predicted by those trying to plot the religious future of this generation. Certainly many baby boomers flirted with meditation, Eastern mysticism, and paranormal phenomena. But that was in their youth. Who would have predicted their acceptance and promotion of the New Age movement?

Although it may be tempting to write off the New Age movement as merely a collection of aging hippies and spiritual experimentalists, the demographics suggest otherwise. The New Age movement is attracting doctors, lawyers, businessmen, politicians, and teachers. And they are actively promoting New Age ideas in every arena with a measure of success.

WHAT IS THE NEW AGE MOVEMENT?

In order to understand its influence, we first need to understand what the New Age is. That is a more difficult task than one might imagine. The movement is eclectic and diverse. The lack of a cohesive movement makes it difficult to define the New Age precisely. The unifying factors are shared ideology rather than a shared organizational structure. And even that is sometimes ineffective because the movement emphasizes and encourages change. The New Age movement is syncretistic and therefore evolutionary in nature. Many proponents change their perspectives, so it is frequently difficult to pin down the major beliefs of this movement.

Nevertheless, there are a number of core beliefs that are important. Here are six major characteristics that people in the New Age have in common:[23]

1. *Monism.* New Agers believe that "all is one." Everything and everyone is interrelated and interdependent. Ultimately

there is no real difference among humans, animals, or God. Any differences between these entities are merely apparent, not real.

2. *Pantheism.* Since New Agers believe that "all is one," the next logical assumption is that "all is god." They teach that all of the universe partakes of the divine essence. All of life has the spark of divinity within.

3. *Human divinity.* The third major tenet of the New Age follows as a logical conclusion from the other two. If "all is one" and "all is god," then "we are gods." We are, according to New Agers, ignorant of our divinity. We are "gods in disguise." The goal, therefore, of the New Age movement is to help us discover our own divinity.

4. *Cosmic consciousness.* Human beings discover their own divinity by experiencing a change in consciousness. According to New Agers, the human race suffers from a collective form of metaphysical amnesia. We have forgotten that our true identity is divine and thus must undergo a change in consciousness to achieve our true human potential.

5. *Reincarnation.* Most New Agers believe in some form of reincarnation. In its classic form, the cycles of birth, death, and reincarnation are necessary to work off our bad karma and to finally reach perfection. The doctrine of karma says that one's present condition was determined by one's actions in a past life. The Western version of reincarnation places less emphasis on bad karma and postulates an upward spiral toward perfection through reincarnation.

6. *Moral relativism.* New Agers think in terms of gray, rather than black or white. Denying the law of noncontradiction, New Agers frequently believe that two conflicting statements can both be true. They will therefore teach that "all religions are true" and that "there are many paths to God."

WHY IS THE NEW AGE MOVEMENT GROWING?
The growth of the New Age movement is directly tied to its basic tenets. New Age theology provides for its followers "a form of godliness"[24] but does not require direct obedience to a transcendent God. It provides spirituality without requiring commitment to spiritual truth. To a generation looking for spirituality but skeptical of the church and religious institutions, the New Age movement has become the answer.

New Age theology appeals to all individuals generally, and to the baby boom generation specifically. It appeals to all of us because it teaches that we are gods and can reach our total human potential by recovering from our metaphysical amnesia and accepting that we have a divine spark within.

New Age theology also is appealing because it teaches that we can control our destinies. We live in a world that seems out of control. The New Age offers not only divinity but human control over our present life and future lives. New Age seminars promise that we can increase our creativity, increase our productivity, decrease our stress, and influence our cosmic destiny.

Finally, New Age theology appeals to us because it offers insight. Through New Age techniques, we can supposedly discover our identities in past lives. The process of "psychic genealogy" offers both adventure and insight. We can explore our souls in previous incarnations, and that exploration might provide clues to our personalities.

Those are general reasons that the New Age movement is growing. The greatest growth has come from the baby boom generation. Their religious perceptions and attitudes differ in at least three ways from those of previous generations: loyalty, traditionality, and morality. And those three differences also explain why the New Age movement is growing among the baby boom generation.

First, baby boomers are cynical. Reared during the tumultuous 1960s, the baby boom generation tends to be distrustful of nearly every institution, including the church.[25] Their parents may have been Presbyterians, but there is no guarantee that they will be Presbyterians or even that they will attend church at all. Boomers look for spirituality where they can find it. Often they believe they have found it at a New Age seminar or within the covers of a book written from a New Age perspective.

Second, baby boomers are unconventional. They don't always look for spiritual values in traditional religion. They are willing to experiment and look for religious significance through the spiritual cafeteria offered in the New Age.

Returning to our previous discussion of religious subcultures, we find statistical support for boomers' adoption of unconventional religious ideas. Nearly half (49 percent) of those identified in the dropout religious subculture believe "God is within us" and more than a third (36 percent) believe in reincarnation. One-fifth of loyalists and returnees believe in astrology, and 36 percent of dropouts believe in astrology.[26] Even those who regularly attend church, and especially those who do not, hold to unorthodox beliefs and may be engaged in unconventional religious practices.

Third, baby boomers generally accept a new morality. Many members of this generation have had a difficult time reconciling their progressive lifestyles with traditional values. The New Age movement allows them to develop their own moral code while still adopting a form of spirituality.

The growth of the New Age movement is due, in large measure, to its ability to attract the spiritually hungry and institutionally cynical. Although the New Age may seem to meet those spiritual needs effectively, the spiritual perspective of the New Age is significantly different from a biblical perspective.

A BIBLICAL PERSPECTIVE OF THE NEW AGE

When the tenets of the New Age movement are examined, one realizes that they are not really new at all. They include aspects of Eastern mysticism and even aspects of occult philosophy. Let's return to those six major characteristics and evaluate them from the biblical perspective.

1. *Monism.* A Christian view of reality rejects the concept of monism. The Bible teaches that God's creation is not an undivided unity but a diversity of created things and beings. The creation is not unified in itself but is held together by Christ in whom "all things hold together."[27]

2. *Pantheism.* Christianity is theistic, not pantheistic. The New Age teaches that God is an impersonal force, whereas the Bible teaches that God is an imminent, personal, triune, sovereign God. God is separate from His creation rather than merely a part of the creation as pantheism would teach.

3. *Human divinity.* Humans are created in God's image and therefore have dignity and value.[28] We are not gods, but we worship the one, true God.

4. *Cosmic consciousness.* New Agers often dabble in the occult in an attempt to achieve a change in consciousness. Although such practices are frequently described in benign terms, such as parapsychology, they involve direct contact with spiritual entities. The Bible warns against the danger of such practices and lists activities such as divination and spirit channeling as detestable practices which are to be avoided.[29]

5. *Reincarnation.* The Bible teaches the resurrection of the body, not reincarnation of the soul.[30] Likewise, the doctrine of karma teaches a concept foreign to the gospel. Salvation comes from grace, not through works in this life or in any other alleged past life.[31] We are not reborn after death. The Bible teaches that "it is appointed for men to die once and after this comes judgement."[32]

6. *Moral relativism.* The Bible teaches absolute truth. God has communicated His moral law, which we are to obey.[33] Contrary to the New Age teaching that "there are many paths to God," Jesus taught "I am the way, the truth and the life. No one comes to the Father except through me."[34]

THE CHALLENGE FOR THE CHRISTIAN CHURCH

Spiritually hungry boomers looking for nourishment for their souls have already tried and will continue to try various menus in America's spiritual cafeteria. Lonely, isolated in boxes in the suburbs, often living hundreds of miles from family, boomers are facing significant psychological issues in the midst of busy lives that sap their emotional and spiritual resources. Beneath that isolation and turmoil is a restless desire for spirituality.

Some will try to meet those needs by dabbling in the New Age movement. And if the churches do not meet their real and perceived needs, that trickle may turn into a torrent. The New Age movement is attractive to the spiritually naive and institutionally cynical. If the church fails, then the New Age will thrive.

This may be the greatest challenge for the Christian church. Can church leaders return baby boomers to the flock? Can the church challenge boomers to a greater level of religious commitment in their lives? Can the church provide the religious training necessary to keep boomers' faith vital? These are important questions.

So far, a significant percentage has not returned to church, and many who have returned seem to view the church as merely one more stop on their itinerary. George Barna says that "having tasted and tried other New Age and materialistic options, a fair number of boomers are returning to the church in search of something real. It's another stop on their journey but hopefully, it will also be the last."[35] The challenge for the church is to be the last stop by providing meaningful answers and by calling this generation to discipleship. That is no small task to serve a generation known for its low commitment and serial conversions.

FAITH AND COMMITMENT

Churches need to challenge boomers to deeper faith and greater religious commitment, but surveys and statistics show that churches themselves may be suffering from the same maladies as baby boomers. Church members like to believe that they are more spiritually committed and live lives different from the unchurched. The data, however, show otherwise.

Approximately 40 percent of America attends church or other religious services on a fairly regular basis. But George Gallup has found that fewer than 10 percent of Americans are deeply committed Christians. Those who are committed "are a breed apart. They are more tolerant of people of diverse backgrounds. They are more involved in charitable activities. They are more involved in practical Christianity. They are absolutely committed to prayer."[36]

Numerous surveys show that most Americans who profess Christianity don't know the basic teachings of the faith. George Gallup stated, "That's the central weakness of Christianity in this country today. There is not a sturdiness of belief. There is a lack of knowledge of Christianity, a lack of awareness of Christian doctrines of atonement, redemption and grace. Many Americans don't have a grasp of these things, and yet eight out of every ten say they are Christians."[37]

Such shallow spirituality makes boomers more susceptible to the latest fad, trend, or religious cult. Gallup notes that not being grounded in the faith means they "are open for anything that comes along." Studies show that New Age beliefs "are just as strong among traditionally religious people as among those who are not traditionally religious."[38]

In many ways the belief system of Christians is not much different than the belief system of society in general. Take just one relevant statistic: belief in absolute truth. George Barna asked Americans if they agreed or disagreed with the statement "There is no such thing as absolute truth." Two-thirds (67 percent) of those surveyed agreed or strongly agreed with that statement. Although one would expect Christians to differ markedly in their response, still a majority (52 percent) of those who claimed to be born-again Christians agreed or strongly agreed with that statement.[39] One has to wonder how effective Christians will be in asserting biblical principles based upon an absolute standard of morality when they say they do not believe that absolute truth exists.

What is true for Christian belief is also true for Christian behavior. Differences between the churched and the unchurched are not as significant as one might imagine. Gallup asked these two groups about their ethics (e.g., likelihood of cheating on income taxes, embellishing résumés). He found that the churched "are just as likely as the unchurched to engage in unethical behavior."[40]

Lack of commitment to a faith position or to a lifestyle based upon biblical principles also extends to church attendance and instruction. Eight in ten Americans believe they can arrive at their own religious views without the help of the church.[41] Apparently church attendance and instruction in the Bible are considered optional by a large majority of Americans.

And when Americans do show up at church their commitment to a particular denomination is even less significant. Nearly 25 percent of American adults have switched religious affiliation at least once.[42] Reasons for the switch vary. The largest percentage switch due to marriage to someone of another faith. Other reasons include: preferring the religious teaching of the new church and relocating to a new community.

And finally, commitment to biblical instruction is not high either. George Gallup says that Americans are trying to do the impossible by "being Christians without the Bible." He goes on to say, "We revere the Bible, but we don't read it."[43] Pastors and pollsters alike have been astounded by the level of biblical illiteracy in this nation. Churches that reach out to baby boomers will no doubt have to shore up their own spiritual commitment as they challenge this generation to a higher level of commitment and discipleship.

CHURCHES AND BABY BOOMERS

The return of this generation to church has not been uniform. Certain denominations and certain types of church structure have been more successful at attracting baby boomers than others. That has, in fact, been another significant challenge to the church: to reach out to this generation on its own terms while still maintaining an internal commitment to spiritual truth.

Some of the changes necessary for outreach are merely common sense, such as providing high-quality child care during worship services. But many others raise profound questions about

Appeal for Boomers

Churches attract baby boomers by:

- emphasizing contemporary music
- providing high-quality child care
- offering short sermons related to everyday life
- offering lots of options for classes and programs
- making low-pressure appeals for membership or money
- getting new members to participate in leadership
- promoting self-fulfillment from religion
- mixing evangelism with interest in social concerns

Source: "A Movable Faith," *Dallas Times Herald*, February 11, 1990.

whether the biblical message is being compromised. And churches today are involved in no small debate about what has come to be known as "the church growth movement."

Much of the debate in the 1980s focused on the Christian right. In the 1990s, debate about the church growth movement has all but overshadowed the political debate. In a sense, the cry has effectively changed from "mobilize" to "modernize." Church growth leaders and their disciples are crying for more relevant churches with more effective worship and evangelism to reach out to seekers. Church growth techniques and church management seminars have become the latest fad.

There is nothing intrinsically wrong with management techniques based upon those principles. After all, John Wesley's followers came to be known as Methodists because of their organizational methods and personal discipline. But in a culture that already lauds style over substance and technique over philosophy, church leaders must be careful to evaluate the goals and methodology of the church growth movement. In an effort to reach a generation already deficient in commitment, churches that adapt a methodology that attempts to make Christianity relevant could easily slip into further compromise.

However, church leaders can err on the other side by refusing to find avenues of ministry by which to reach out to this generation. Missionaries traveling to foreign lands study a culture and the particular needs and perspectives of people in that culture. They are well aware that establishing a church depends upon meeting needs and clearly communicating the gospel to the people in that culture in an effective way. So it is with the baby boom generation and its particular "culture."

Churches that are successfully reaching baby boomers have a number of things in common. For example, they provide practical teaching, emphasize healthy relationships, are less formal, and are action-oriented. None of those traits necessarily represents a compromise of the message of the gospel, but they can lead to compromise if not prudently applied. This, again, is the great challenge to the church today. Church leaders must constantly work to find effective ways to reach out to baby boomers while still maintaining a commitment to spiritual truth.

What are baby boomers looking for, and how can the church effectively, without compromise, meet those needs? Here are a number of things that baby boomers want and how the church can meet some of their needs:

1. *Teaching that is relevant and practical.* It has often been said that for every person worrying about the end of the world there are a thousand people worrying about the end of the month. Baby boomers are no different. They are impatient with abstract, theoretical analysis. This generation wants to know how every issue (including spiritual issues) affects them on a daily basis. They want frank, honest, practical messages and discussions about priorities, pressures, and temptations.

2. *Personal involvement.* Boomers want to participate in the process. They want to take part in worship, instruction, and fellowship. They also want to be a part of decision making and will take responsibility.

This is a "hands on" generation. They have largely been responsible for the 600 percent increase in the number of private business ventures in the last thirty years.[44] They are entrepreneurs who want a stake in the action, whether it is in the business world or in the church.

3. *Social concern and involvement.* In many ways, the 1960s mentality is still current in the 1990s. This generation is still socially involved. Widely diverse groups such as ACT-UP, Earth First, Operation Rescue, and Promise Keepers testify to the continuing social concern of boomers from various political and theological positions. Reaching out to the society is a part of this generation's mind-set. Ministry must be based not merely on word but on deed.

Ten Traits Common to Churches
That Are Reaching Baby Boomers:

1. They are open to a spiritual experience.
2. Their Bible teaching stresses practical living.
3. They place a healthy emphasis on relationships.
4. They have fewer titles and less formality.
5. They understand the new family in America.
6. They share their faith by what they say and do.
7. They recognize the ability of women.
8. They place an emphasis on worship.
9. They have a high tolerance for diversity.
10. They are action-oriented.

Source: Jack Sims, "Why Are These People Smiling? Because They Don't Have
          to Go to Church Anymore" (Lecture at Fuller Theological Seminary,
          Pasadena, California).

4. *Intellectual challenge.* The best educated generation in history does not want simplistic answers to tough, complex questions. An appeal to authority or an occasional Bible verse is not enough to satisfy the intellectual struggle and journey of a generation looking for spiritual answers.

5. *Experience oriented.* On the other hand, boomers are interested in churches that do more than just feed the mind. They need to experience God and spiritual truth themselves, not just learn about it vicariously. They also need high touch to go along with their high tech world. This generation grew up in a mass culture that is increasingly impersonal. They are looking for feelings and a personal, spiritual experience.

6. *Answers for their pain and problems.* This generation is experiencing a high level of dysfunctionality and is more aware of its psychological and spiritual problems than other generations seemed to be. They want churches to acknowledge and minister to their problems. But they don't want clichés or psychobabble. They want real, meaningful, effective answers.

7. *Recognition of the changing family.* Churches have traditionally focused most (if not all) of their attention on families with children. Singles, divorced, and couples without children, to mention just a few, often do not feel there is a place for them in

church. Boomers expect churches to reach out to the changing family structure in America.

8. *Role for women.* Changing roles for women in society have left boomer women eager for additional responsibility within the church. Women who exercise their gifts and talents in the workplace are not content to only serve in the nursery. They also expect to be appreciated for their abilities.

The application of these principles will no doubt vary from church to church. And church leaders must be careful to reach out to this generation in an effective way that does not compromise the gospel message. Just as missionaries must carefully evaluate their strategies to reach out to a foreign culture, so church leaders must be careful to evaluate their outreach to the baby boom culture.

SMALL GROUPS AND BABY BOOMERS

One of the most effective ways to reach out to baby boomers is outside the walls of the church building. Small groups provide opportunities for meeting needs and building bridges that often will not occur within a formal worship service. The psychographics of this generation suggests that small groups are an effective way to meet their needs.

1. *Baby boomers are cynical.* Two pivotal events in the lives of baby boomers were the civil rights movement and the Vietnam War. Whereas the civil rights movement was the source of this generation's idealism, the Vietnam War provided its cynicism. Scandals in politics, media, business, and religion have reinforced cynicism toward institutions, including the church. Many baby boomers will not even go into a church structure, especially those in the spiritual subculture known as dropouts.

But even though they may be generally cynical and distrustful of institutions, boomers will respond to one-on-one relationships and small group opportunities if they perceive them as genuine expressions of love and concern. Small groups can be an effective entry point for spiritual discussions and ministry.

2. *Baby boomers are secular.* Baby boomers are less involved in organized religion than their parents are for many reasons. First, as already noted, they are distrustful of institutions, including the church. Second, boomers spent more years in educational pursuits than any other generation. Most of their education has

taken place in secular arenas that have been either ambivalent toward or even hostile to Christian values.

Finally, baby boomers find themselves living in a secular world dominated by secular ideas. Sociologist Peter Berger uses an intriguing metaphor to describe this circumstance. One of the most religious countries in the world is India, and the least religious country is Sweden. Baby boomers find themselves in a culture Berger describes as a nation of Indians ruled by Swedes. Those in positions of authority (education, media, politics, business) are generally secular in their outlook, so baby boomers do not know how religion fits into their lives.

Boomers, therefore, do not see the local church as relevant, nor do they see it as a source of answers to their problems. Only 22 percent identify themselves as born-again Christians.[45] Going to a church service is irrelevant to many and even forbidding to some. A small group meeting in a home, on the other hand, is much less threatening than a church service. Groups which allow them to meet neighbors and discuss issues of importance to them may provide a means to overcome some of their emotional and intellectual hurdles.

3. *Baby boomers are less committed.* Commitment to friends, relatives, marriage, even church does not always come easily. Many Sunday school teachers wonder if they taught the same message two Sundays in a row if anyone but a small minority would notice. So many couples are transient that maintaining continuity between lessons is nearly impossible. The problem is even worse in singles' and career classes. Small groups can provide some of that continuity.

Small groups can also provide accountability. It is easy to get lost in a large church or Sunday school class. It is more difficult to "blend into the crowd" in a small group of eight to twelve people. A person's absence is felt and lack of preparation becomes obvious in a small group. The accountability of the group can significantly increase commitment.

4. *Baby boomers are lonely.* The "crisis of loneliness" discussed previously strikes both singles and couples. The number of childless single-person households increase every year. Add to that single-parent households and couples experiencing "living-together loneliness," and you have a virtual epidemic of lonely people. Whether single or in a relationship, members of this generation have a crying need for fellowship and intimacy.

Small groups can provide a context for fellowship and ministry. Boomers frazzled by their frenetic, fast-paced lifestyles can find comfort from others in their group. Members of small groups often say they are closer to members of their small group than they are to their own families. When a member has a need, others rally to provide meals, prayer support, or do whatever is needed. Small groups can provide a point of contact and a cultural context missing in this fast-paced society.

5. *Baby boomers are distracted.* Most boomers live very busy lives. They may be disciplined in their careers, but they rarely take the time to apply various disciplines to their lives.

A small group context provides an opportunity to talk and to apply biblical principles. It isn't enough to hear a message. To apply a message to our lives we must be held accountable to others. Small groups can assure that baby boom believers become not merely "hearers," but also "doers of the Word."

The boom generation does face a crisis of spirituality. As boomers collectively pass through midlife, they look to the future with more anxiety than anticipation. Questions about identity and significance are on their minds. They are lonely and isolated as they go about their busy lives. Beneath that isolation and turmoil is a restless desire for spirituality. Their needs and questions must be addressed on a spiritual level. They are not easily answered in a secular world nor in a mystical world filled with bland spirituality.

This educated generation will look for a church that can clearly articulate its beliefs and provide satisfying answers. This emotionally needy generation will look for a church that listens and ministers to those needs. This socially-conscious generation will look for a church that is socially aware and making an impact on its community.

If it finds such churches, it will most likely stay and worship and minister. If it does not, then it will move on, looking for other places to find answers and fulfill needs. In short, if the church fails, the New Age will thrive.

NOTES

1. Wade Clark Roof, "The Baby Boom's Search for God," *American Demographics*, December 1992, 54.

2. Os Guinness, *The Gravedigger File* (Downers Grove, Ill.: InterVarsity, 1983), 51.

3. Roof, "Baby Boom's Search," 54.

4. Guinness, *Gravedigger File*, 96.

5. George Sim Johnston, "Break Glass in Case of Emergency," *Beyond the Boom: New Voices on American Life, Culture, and Politics*, ed. Terry Teachout (New York: Poseidon, 1990), 55.

6. Faith Popcorn, *Adweek's Marketing Week*, May 18, 1987, 12.

7. Ken Sidey, "A Generation on the Doorstep," *Moody*, January 1987, 22.

8. These categories were devised by Roof in "Baby Boom's Search," 50–57.

9. Ibid., 56.

10. George Gallup and Jim Castelli, *The People's Religion* (New York: Macmillan, 1989), 66–67.

11. Roof, "Baby Boom's Search," 55.

12. Ken Woodward, "A Time to Seek," *Newsweek*, December 17, 1990, 51.

13. Gallup and Castelli, *People's Religion*, 132–48.

14. "Despite the Great Return, All the Pews Aren't Full," *Newsweek*, December 17, 1990, 54.

15. Sidey, "Generation on the Doorstep," 23.

16. William Greider, "Portrait of a Generation," *Rolling Stone*, April 7, 1988, 38.

17. Wesley Pippert, "A Generation Warms to Religion," *Christianity Today*, October 6, 1989, 22.

18. Ibid.

19. Ibid.

20. Ibid., 23.

21. "Religion, Spirituality and American Families," survey conducted by *Better Homes and Gardens*, 1988.

22. Johnston, "Break Glass," 59.

23. Doug Groothuis, *Unmasking the New Age* (Downers Grove, Ill.: InterVarsity, 1986).

24. 2 Timothy 3:5.

25. Paul Light, *Baby Boomers* (New York: Norton, 1988).

26. Roof, "Baby Boom's Search," 56.

27. Colossians 1:17.

28. Genesis 1:27; Psalm 8.

29. Deuteronomy 18:9–13.

30. 1 Corinthians 15.

31. Ephesians 2:8–9.

32. Hebrews 9:27.

33. Exodus 20:1–17.

34. John 14:6.

35. Quoted in Paula Rinehart, "The Pivotal Generation," *Christianity Today*, October 6, 1989, 21.

36. "Fewer Than 10% of Americans Are Deeply Committed Christians," *National and International Religion Report*, May 20, 1991, 1.

37. "Tracking America's Soul," *Christianity Today*, November 17, 1989, 24.

38. "Deeply Committed Christians," 1.

39. George Barna, *What Americans Believe: An Annual Survey of Values and Religious Views in the United States* (Ventura, Calif.: Regal, 1991) 84-85.

40. "Deeply Committed Christians," 1.

41. Robert Bellah, *Habits of the Heart* (New York: Harper & Row, 1985), 221.

42. "Nearly 25% of U.S. Adults Have Switched Religious Affiliation at Least Once," *National and International Religion Report*, June 29, 1992, 1.

43. "Gallup Tells Editors: American Revere the Bible, Don't Read It," *World*, May 19, 1990, 8.

44. Rinehart, "Pivotal Generation," 25.

45. Greider, "Portrait of a Generation," 34.

EPILOGUE

As the baby boom generation, and those born after it, head toward the twenty-first century, they will encounter many of the crises described in this book. If you have not already experienced some in-flight turbulence, you certainly will. These uniform crises will affect all of us in one way or another.

Even more disturbing is the plain fact that these crises will occur in a society caught in the throes of significant change. The forces of these changes (social, economic, political, psychological, moral, spiritual) have already altered our societal landscape in ways that make our world vastly different and more complex than the world of just a few decades ago.

Crises in the midst of constant change is scary and undermines our ability to adapt and cope. But cope and change we must. This is the lesson of the Latin phrase *tempora mutantur nos et mutamur in illus*—"times change and we change with them." We can change and alter the force and direction of many of these crises. Either we deal with the social, psychological, economic, and spiritual issues now or we will pay the consequences later.

Effectively meeting this challenge requires at least two things. First, you must truly understand the problem. This book has intentionally been long on diagnosis and short on prescription. Knowing that crisis and change are coming is crucial to adapting and adjusting. Being forewarned allows you to be forearmed about these coming crises that will change your life.

Obviously, there are general prescriptions each of us should follow. These would include such things as building relationships, establishing priorities, getting out of debt, attending church services. But the individual applications of even those general principles is as varied as the number of people reading this book. Differences in age, gender, marital status, family situation, and religious convictions preclude a simple answer.

Second, meeting this challenge also requires a firm basis of convictions. We need to build our lives on a firm foundation when so much around us is shifting sand. As a Christian I believe that Jesus Christ is that foundation and that a Christian world and life view provides an accurate perspective to evaluate the world and ourselves. If we are to understand the changing social landscape, then we must have an accurate picture of the world. And if we are to adapt to those changes, then we must understand ourselves. While we might find answers to the first question in social statistics and analysis, we will find accurate answers to the second only in the timeless truths found in the Bible.

My goal in this book has been to provide insight and information that will enable you to analyze your individual circumstances. Hopefully this book has provided you with a perspective that will help you anticipate these crises and react accordingly. If you would like more information or perspective, please write to me: Kerby Anderson, P.O. Box 2050, Dallas, TX 75221. I will try to provide additional information, updated statistics, newsletters, slides, speeches, and so on as time and resources allow.

The message of this book is hopeful. You can make a difference if you understand the changes that have already altered our societal landscape and prepare for the coming crises that will inevitably change your life.